GREEK TEMPLES

THE METROPOLITAN MUSEUM OF ART

GREEK TEMPLES

BY
ISABEL HOOPES GRINNELL

NEW YORK · 1943

IN planning and assembling material for this book the articles and lectures of Professor William B. Dinsmoor, as well as important suggestions made by Lucy T. Shoe, have been of great value. The writer also wishes to acknowledge with gratitude the assistance of Walter Hauser, who was kind enough to read the present manuscript, and the editorial work of Georgiana Remer and Jean Leonard.

The plans and drawings in the text and the drawing on the title page, the façade of the Temple of Artemis at Corfu, were made by Lindsley F. Hall. The photograph of the Parthenon on the cover was taken by Saul S. Weinberg.

COPYRIGHT BY THE METROPOLITAN MUSEUM OF ART, 1943

CONTENTS

	PAGE
LIST OF PLATES	vii
INTRODUCTION	xv
THE TEMPLE OF APOLLO THERMIOS AT THERMON	1
THE TEMPLE OF HERA AT OLYMPIA	3
THE TEMPLE OF ARTEMIS AT EPHESOS	5
THE TEMPLE OF ATHENA (?) AT ASSOS	8
THE TEMPLE OF APOLLO AT CORINTH	10
THE OLD TEMPLE OF ATHENA AT ATHENS	12
THE TEMPLE OF APOLLO AT DELPHI	14
THE TEMPLE OF APHAIA AT AIGINA	17
THE TEMPLE OF HERA, OR THE TEMPLE E-R, AT SELINUS	20
THE TEMPLE OF ZEUS OLYMPIOS AT AKRAGAS (AGRIGENTUM)	22
THE TEMPLE OF ZEUS AT OLYMPIA	25
THE "TEMPLE OF POSEIDON" AT POSEIDONIA (PAESTUM)	28
THE TEMPLE OF APOLLO EPIKOURIOS AT BASSAI	30
THE TEMPLE OF HEPHAISTOS AT ATHENS (FORMERLY CALLED THE THESEION)	32
THE PARTHENON AT ATHENS	34
THE TEMPLE OF POSEIDON AT SOUNION	38
THE TEMPLE AT EGESTA (SEGESTA)	40
THE TEMPLE OF ATHENA NIKE AT ATHENS	42
THE ARGIVE HERAION	44
THE ERECHTHEION AT ATHENS	46
THE TEMPLE OF ASKLEPIOS AT EPIDAUROS	49
THE TEMPLE OF ATHENA ALEA AT TEGEA	51

THE TEMPLE OF ARTEMIS AT SARDIS	53
THE TEMPLE OF APOLLO AT DIDYMA	55
THE TEMPLE OF ZEUS OLYMPIOS AT ATHENS	57
KEY TO ABBREVIATIONS USED IN FOOTNOTES AND REFERENCES	59
GLOSSARY	59
PLATES	61

LIST OF PLATES

PLATE I. THE TEMPLE OF APOLLO THERMIOS AT THERMON—DORIC
- A. Terracotta Antefixes. In the National Museum, Athens. *Antike Denkmäler*, II, pl. 53.
- B. A Restoration of the Polychrome Entablature. *Ibid.*, pl. 49.
- C. The Present State of the Temple. Photograph by H. Wagner.

PLATE II. THE TEMPLE OF APOLLO THERMIOS AT THERMON
- A. Terracotta Metope: a Hunter with a Stag and a Boar. In the National Museum, Athens. *Antike Denkmäler*, II, pl. 51.
- B. Terracotta Metope: Perseus. In the National Museum, Athens. *Ibid.*, pl. 51.
- C. Terracotta Metope: Seated Goddesses. In the National Museum, Athens. *Ibid.*, pl. 50.
- D. Terracotta Metope: a Gorgon's Head. In the National Museum, Athens. *Ibid.*, pl. 52.
- E. Terracotta Antefixes. In the National Museum, Athens. *Ibid.*, pl. 53.

PLATE III. THE TEMPLE OF HERA AT OLYMPIA—DORIC
- A. The Roof Construction. The Roof Was Made of Wood and Terracotta. Curtius and Adler, *Olympia*, Plates, II, pl. LXXXXVIII.
- B. Types of Capitals. Gardiner, *Olympia*, fig. 56.
- C. The East Façade of the Temple as Drawn by Adler. Curtius and Adler, *Olympia*, Plates, II, pl. LXXXIV.

PLATE IV. THE TEMPLE OF HERA AT OLYMPIA
- A. A Restoration of a Terracotta Gable Akroterion. Curtius and Adler, *Olympia*, Plates, II, pl. CXV.
- B. A Head of Hera, Probably from the Cult Statue. In the Olympia Museum. Curtius and Adler, *Olympia*, Plates, III, pl. I.
- C. The Present State of the Temple. Photograph by Walter Hege.

PLATE V. THE TEMPLE OF ARTEMIS AT EPHESOS—IONIC
- A. A Restoration of the Western End of the Archaic Temple. Hogarth, *Excavations at Ephesos*, Atlas, pl. XIII.
- B. A View of the West Portico of the Archaic Temple from the South, as Restored by F. Krischen. The Position of the Sculptured Drums Is Conjectural. F. Krischen, *Die griechische Stadt* (Berlin, 1938), pl. 33.

PLATE VI. THE TEMPLE OF ARTEMIS AT EPHESOS
- A. Fragments of the Drums of the Archaic Temple. In the British Museum. Photograph by Mansell.
- B. A Sculptured Drum from the Later Temple. In the British Museum. Photograph by Mansell.
- C. A Restoration of the West Front of the Later Temple with the Drums Wrongly Superimposed. Anderson, Spiers, and Dinsmoor, *Architecture of Ancient Greece*, pl. L.

LIST OF PLATES

PLATE VII. THE TEMPLE OF ATHENA (?) AT ASSOS—DORIC
- A. A Restoration of the East Front. The Decoration Was Differently Arranged. Clarke, Bacon, and Koldewey, *Investigations at Assos*, p. 145.
- B. A Detail of the Mosaic Pavement. *Ibid.*, p. 164, fig. 1.
- C. The Construction. *Ibid.*, p. 157, fig. 5.

PLATE VIII. THE TEMPLE OF ATHENA (?) AT ASSOS
- A and B. Details of the Architrave Decoration. In the Museum of Fine Arts, Boston. Photographs Courtesy of the Museum of Fine Arts, Boston.
- C. The Akropolis at Assos Seen from the Sea. Clarke, Bacon, and Koldewey, *Investigations at Assos*, p. 15, fig. 1.

PLATE IX. THE TEMPLE OF APOLLO AT CORINTH—DORIC
- A. The Temple as Drawn by Stuart in 1751. Stuart and Revett, *Antiquities of Athens*, III, pl. XLII.
- B. The Temple as Drawn by H. W. Williams in 1818. Fowler and Stillwell, *Corinth*, I, fig. 92.

PLATE X. THE TEMPLE OF APOLLO AT CORINTH
- A. A Comparison of the Orders of the Temples of Apollo at Corinth and Delphi and the Old Temple of Athena in Athens. Fowler and Stillwell, *Corinth*, I, fig. 88.
- B. A View from the South with Restored Stereobate. Photograph by Saul S. Weinberg.
- C. A View from the East. Photograph by Walter Hauser.

PLATE XI. THE OLD TEMPLE OF ATHENA ON THE AKROPOLIS AT ATHENS—DORIC
- A. A Restoration of the Early Temple in Antis with the Outline of the Peisistratid Temple. Details of the Famous Pedimental Figures, Wrongly Placed Here, Are Shown on the Opposite Page. Wiegand, *Die archaische Porosarchitektur der Akropolis zu Athen*, fig. 112.
- B. A Restoration of a Corner of the Small Temple in Antis. *Ibid.*, fig. 24.
- C. A Restoration of a Corner of the Peisistratid Temple. *Ibid.*, fig. 118.

PLATE XII. THE OLD TEMPLE OF ATHENA ON THE AKROPOLIS AT ATHENS
- A. Athena and a Giant from the Peisistratid Temple. In the Akropolis Museum. Photograph by Alinari.
- B. Head of a Monster. In the Akropolis Museum. Photograph by Walter Hege.
- C. Herakles and the Triton. In the Akropolis Museum. Hege, *Die Akropolis*, fig. 2.
- D. Head of Herakles, Found in 1938. In the Akropolis Museum. *Hesperia*, VIII (1939), fig. 5.
- E. The Present State of the Temple with the Erechtheion Beyond and the City Below, Taken from the Parthenon. Photograph by Walter Hege.

PLATE XIII. THE TEMPLE OF APOLLO AT DELPHI—DORIC
- A and B. Restorations of the Temple in the Early VI Century B.C. and in the Late IV Century B.C. Courby, *Fouilles de Delphes*, II, part 1, figs. 156 and 157.
- C. A Model of Delphi as It Was in the II Century A.D., Made by Hans Schleif. In the Metropolitan Museum.

LIST OF PLATES

PLATE XIV. THE TEMPLE OF APOLLO AT DELPHI
- A. A Lion Devouring a Hind, from the East Pediment of the Alkmeonid Temple. In the Delphi Museum. Photograph by Alinari.
- B. Akroterion (center) and Figures from the East Pediment of the Alkmeonid Temple. In the Delphi Museum. Picard and de la Coste-Messelière, *Sculptures grecques de Delphes*, pl. XXXIV.
- C. A View of the Remains of the Temple from Mount Parnassos.

PLATE XV. THE TEMPLE OF APHAIA AT AIGINA—DORIC
- A. A Restoration of the East Front and a Section through the Pediment. Furtwängler, *Aegina*, pl. 33.
- B. The Construction. *Ibid.*, pl. 36.

PLATE XVI. THE TEMPLE OF APHAIA AT AIGINA
- A. Athena, from the West Pediment. In the Glyptothek, Munich. *Denkmäler griechischer und römischer Sculptur.*
- B. Herakles, from the East Pediment. In the Glyptothek, Munich. Photograph by C. Kennedy.
- C. A Fallen Warrior, from the East Pediment. In the Glyptothek, Munich. *Denkmäler griechischer und römischer Sculptur.*
- D. The Interior of the Temple. Photograph by H. Wagner.

PLATE XVII. THE TEMPLE OF HERA, OR THE TEMPLE E-R, AT SELINUS—DORIC
- A. A Restoration of the East Front. Hulot and Fougères, *Sélinonte*, p. 260.
- B. A Metope: the Marriage of Zeus and Hera. In the Museo Nazionale, Palermo. Photograph by Alinari.

PLATE XVIII. THE TEMPLE OF HERA, OR THE TEMPLE E-R, AT SELINUS
- A. A Metope: Herakles Fighting an Amazon. In the Museo Nazionale, Palermo. Photograph by Alinari.
- B. The Present State of the Temple. Randall-MacIver, *Greek Cities in Italy and Sicily*, pl. xx.

PLATE XIX. THE TEMPLE OF ZEUS OLYMPIOS AT AKRAGAS (AGRIGENTUM)—DORIC
- A. A Section Showing the Inner Pilasters and the Means of Hoisting Blocks. Stuart and Revett, *Antiquities of Athens*, IV, pl. V.
- B. A Restoration of a Corner of the Temple Showing the Position of the Colossal Figures. Koldewey and Puchstein, *Die griechischen Tempel in Unteritalien und Sicilien*, I, fig. 143.
- C. A Restoration of the Façade by Cockerell Showing the Comparative Sizes of this Temple and the Parthenon. The Exact Height Is Conjectural. Stuart and Revett, *Antiquities of Athens*, IV, pl. II.

PLATE XX. THE TEMPLE OF ZEUS OLYMPIOS AT AKRAGAS
- A. Part of the North Side of the Temple at the End of the XIX Century. Koldewey and Puchstein, *Die griechischen Tempel in Unteritalien und Sicilien*, I, fig. 138.
- B. The Head of One of the Colossal Figures. *Bolletino d'arte*, series II, VI (1926–1927), p. 42, fig. 14.
- C. An Atlante and a Corner of the North Wall of the Temple. Photograph by Lucy T. Shoe.

LIST OF PLATES

PLATE XXI. THE TEMPLE OF ZEUS AT OLYMPIA—DORIC
- A. The East Pediment as Restored by Studniczka. The Sculptures Are in the Olympia Museum.
- B. The West Pediment as Restored by Treu. The Sculptures Are in the Olympia Museum.
- C. Longitudinal Section. Curtius and Adler, *Olympia*, Plates, I, pl. XII.
- D. A Model of Olympia as It Appeared in the II Century A.D., Made by Hans Schleif. In the Metropolitan Museum.

PLATE XXII. THE TEMPLE OF ZEUS AT OLYMPIA
- A. A Corner of the Entablature Showing the Roof Construction. Curtius and Adler, *Olympia*, Plates, I, pl. XVI.
- B. Restorations of the East Front and of the Interior, Showing the Conjectural Appearance of the Cult Statue. *Memoirs of the American Academy in Rome*, IV, pls. LIX and LXI.
- C. The Present State of the Temple. Photograph by Walter Hege.

PLATE XXIII. THE TEMPLE OF ZEUS AT OLYMPIA
- A. The Central Group from the West Pediment: Theseus and a Centaur, Apollo, Deidameia and Eurytion. In the Olympia Museum. Photograph by Alinari.
- B.–E. Figures from the East Pediment: "Handmaiden," "Seer," "Alpheios," "Kladeos." In the Olympia Museum. Photographs by Alinari.

PLATE XXIV. THE TEMPLE OF ZEUS AT OLYMPIA
- A–D. Metopes: Herakles and Atlas, the Augean Stable, Herakles and Kerberos, the Stymphalian Birds. In the Olympia Museum. Photographs by Alinari.
- E. Lion-head Waterspouts. In the Olympia Museum. Photograph by Alinari.

PLATE XXV. THE "TEMPLE OF POSEIDON" AT POSEIDONIA (PAESTUM)—DORIC
- A. The Interior, Showing the Second Range of Columns. Photograph by Lindsley F. Hall.
- B. A Restoration of the Interior. Borrman and Neuwirth, *Geschichte der Baukunst*, I, fig. 82.

PLATE XXVI. THE "TEMPLE OF POSEIDON" AT POSEIDONIA
- A. A View of a Corner of the "Basilica" and the Temple. Photograph by Lindsley F. Hall.
- B. The Present State of the Temple. Photograph by Alinari.

PLATE XXVII. THE TEMPLE OF APOLLO EPIKOURIOS AT BASSAI (NEAR PHIGALEIA)—DORIC
- A. A Restoration of the Interior by Dinsmoor. Drawn by Lindsley F. Hall.
- B. The Raking Sima. In the British Museum. Dinsmoor, *Metropolitan Museum Studies*, vol. IV, part 2, fig. 21.
- C. A Detail of the Centaur Frieze. In the British Museum. *Ibid.*, fig. 11.
- D. Herakles, a Detail of the Amazon Frieze. In the British Museum.

PLATE XXVIII. THE TEMPLE OF APOLLO EPIKOURIOS AT BASSAI
- A. The Present State of the Interior. Photograph by Walter Hauser.
- B. A Restoration of the Interior by Cockerell. Cockerell, *Temples . . . at Aegina and . . . Bassae*, p. 59.
- C. The Present State of the Temple. Photograph by Walter Hauser.

LIST OF PLATES

PLATE XXIX. THE TEMPLE OF HEPHAISTOS AT ATHENS (THE THESEION)—DORIC
- A. A Restored Perspective of the Portico Interior, Showing the Frieze. Koch, *Arch. Anz.*, XLIII (1928), p. 711, fig. 3.
- B. A Metope: Herakles and the Cretan Bull. In Situ. Photograph by Alison Frantz.
- C. A Metope: Theseus and Kerkyon. Original in Situ. From a Cast.
- D. A Detail of the Frieze. Original in Situ. From a Cast.

PLATE XXX. THE TEMPLE OF HEPHAISTOS AT ATHENS
- A. The East Front. Photograph by H. Wagner.
- B. The Temple from the Northwest. Photograph by Alinari.

PLATE XXXI. THE PARTHENON AT ATHENS—DORIC
- A. The Eastern Pediment, the Birth of Athena (above), and the Western Pediment, the Contest of Athena and Poseidon, as Drawn in 1674. Omont, *Athènes au XVIIe siècle*, pls. I, II, and III.
- B. A Corner Showing a Metope and an Antefix in Place. Photograph by Walter Hege.
- C. An Athenian Coin of about 200 B.C. with the Head of Athena Parthenos. In the E. T. Newell Collection.
- D. The Varvakeion Statuette, a Copy of the Athena Parthenos in the National Museum, Athens. Photograph by Alinari.

PLATE XXXII. THE PARTHENON AT ATHENS
- A. A View from the Southeast. Photograph by Saul S. Weinberg.
- B. A Detail of the Temple Showing the Position of the Frieze. Photograph by Nellys Studio, Athens.

PLATE XXXIII. THE PARTHENON AT ATHENS
- A and B. Figures from the East Pediment. In the British Museum. Right, the "Fates." Smith, *The Sculptures of the Parthenon*, pls. 4 and 5.
- C. "Theseus," from the East Pediment. In the British Museum. *Ibid.*, pl. 2.
- D. A Group from the West Pediment. In Situ. *Ibid.*, pl. 8.
- E and F. Metopes: Scenes from the Battle of the Lapiths and Centaurs. In the British Museum. *Ibid.*, pls. 22 and 19.

PLATE XXXIV. THE PARTHENON AT ATHENS
- A. Seated Gods from the East Frieze. In the Akropolis Museum. *Les Sculptures du Parthénon*, Editions "Tel," no. 49.
- B. Marshal and Maidens from the East Frieze. In the Louvre. *Ibid.*, no. 50.
- C. Elders from the North Frieze. In the Akropolis Museum. *Ibid.*, no. 42.
- D. Offering Bearers from the North Frieze. In the Akropolis Museum. *Ibid.*, no. 41.
- E. Young Horsemen from the North Frieze. In the British Museum. *Ibid.*, no. 44.
- F. Riders from the West Frieze. In Situ. *Ibid.*, no. 40.

PLATE XXXV. THE TEMPLE OF POSEIDON AT SOUNION—DORIC
- A and B. The Side and Front Elevations Restored. Blouet, *Expédition de Morée*, pl. 37.

LIST OF PLATES

    C. The Frieze and Architrave over an Anta Capital and the Exterior Entablature and Capital. *Ibid.*, pl. 33.

PLATE XXXVI. THE TEMPLE OF POSEIDON AT SOUNION
- A. A View of the Temple from the Northwest. Photograph by Dr. Alexander Forbes.
- B. A Seated Figure, Probably from a Pediment. Ἀρχαιολογικὴ Ἐφημερίς (1917), p. 196, fig. 11.
- C. Looking toward the Sea from the Interior. Photograph by Nellys Studio, Athens.

PLATE XXXVII. THE TEMPLE AT EGESTA (SEGESTA)—DORIC
- A. The Southeast Corner of the Temple. Photograph by Walter Hauser.
- B. The Interior, Looking West. Photograph by Walter Hauser.
- C. A Corner of the Temple as Drawn by Hittorff. Koldewey and Puchstein, *Die griechischen Tempel in Unteritalien und Sicilien*, I, fig. 120.

PLATE XXXVIII. THE TEMPLE AT EGESTA
- A. A View into the Interior from the Southwest Corner. Photograph by Walter Hauser.
- B. A Detail Showing the Bosses and the Curvature of the Stylobate on the South Side. Photograph by Walter Hauser.
- C. The West Front of the Temple. Photograph by Walter Hauser.

PLATE XXXIX. THE TEMPLE OF ATHENA NIKE AT ATHENS—IONIC
- A. The Assembly of Deities, Part of the Frieze. In Situ. Photograph by Walter Hege.
- B and C. Two Nikes from the Parapet Built around the Temple. In the Akropolis Museum. Photograph by Walter Hege.

PLATE XL. THE TEMPLE OF ATHENA NIKE AT ATHENS
- A. A Restoration of the Akropolis Showing the Position of the Temple. D'Ooge, *The Akropolis of Athens*, pl. IX.
- B. The Temple as It Appeared in 1940. *The American Journal of Archaeology*, XLIV (1940), p. 537.

PLATE XLI. THE ARGIVE HERAION—DORIC
- A. A Restoration of the East Front. Waldstein, *The Argive Heraeum*, I, fig. 59.
- B. A Restored Cross Section, Showing the Statue of Hera. *Ibid.*, fig. 53.

PLATE XLII. THE ARGIVE HERAION
- A. A Restoration of the Sima by E. L. Tilton. Waldstein, *The Argive Heraeum*, I, fig. 61.
- B. An Argive Coin with the Head of Hera. In the E. T. Newell Collection.
- C. A Head of Hera, Probably from the West Pediment. In the National Museum, Athens. Waldstein, *The Argive Heraeum*, I, frontispiece.
- D. The Present State of the Temple. Photograph by Frank Walton.

PLATE XLIII. THE ERECHTHEION AT ATHENS—IONIC
- A. A Restoration of the Temple, East Façade. Stevens and Others, *The Erechtheum*, pl. XIII.
- B. A Restoration of the Temple, West Façade. *Ibid.*, pl. XIII.
- C. A Restoration of the North Façade. *Ibid.*, pl. XIV.

LIST OF PLATES

PLATE XLIV. THE ERECHTHEION AT ATHENS
- A. A Group from the Frieze. In the Akropolis Museum, Athens.
- B. The Caryatid Porch. Photograph by Walter Hege.
- C. The Present State of the Temple Seen from the West. Photograph by C. H. Whitaker.

PLATE XLV. THE TEMPLE OF ASKLEPIOS AT EPIDAUROS—DORIC
- A. The Abaton, or Dormitory for Pilgrims. Πρακτικά (1905), fig. 12.
- B. A Restoration of the East Front. Defrasse and Lechat, *Épidaure*, p. 55.

PLATE XLVI. THE TEMPLE OF ASKLEPIOS AT EPIDAUROS
- A. A Relief of Asklepios. In the National Museum, Athens. Photograph by Alinari.
- B. A Nike: an Akroterion. In the National Museum, Athens.
- C. The Theater at Epidauros with the Ruins of the Sanctuary in the Distance at the Left.

PLATE XLVII. THE TEMPLE OF ATHENA ALEA AT TEGEA—DORIC
- A. A Drawing of the East Façade. Dugas, *Le Sanctuaire d'Aléa Athéna à Tegée*, pls. XII–XIV.
- B. Longitudinal Section. *Ibid.*, pls. XVIII–XX.
- C. A Restoration of a Column Base and Base Molding in the Interior. *Ibid.*, pl. LXXV.

PLATE XLVIII. THE TEMPLE OF ATHENA ALEA AT TEGEA
- A. The Head of Herakles from the West Pediment. Original in the Museum at Tegea. From a Cast.
- B. A Capital from the Interior, Restored. In the Museum at Tegea. Dugas, *Le Sanctuaire d'Aléa Athéna à Tegée*, pl. XCI.
- C and D. The Crowning Molding inside the Cella and the Sima. In the Museum at Tegea. *Ibid.*, pls. XCIII and LXXXVI.
- E. A View of the Temple from the East. *Ibid.*, pl. LXXXII.

PLATE XLIX. THE TEMPLE OF ARTEMIS AT SARDIS—IONIC
- A and B. A Restoration of the East End: Longitudinal Section and Transverse Section. Butler, *Sardis*, II, part 1, figs. 101 a, b.
- C. A Suggested Restoration of the West Steps. *Ibid.*, fig. 97.
- D. A Restoration of the Doorway. *Ibid.*, Atlas, pl. III.
- E. A Detail of One of the Columns. *Ibid.*, pl. B.

PLATE L. THE TEMPLE OF ARTEMIS AT SARDIS
- A. A View of the East Porch from the North. Butler, *Sardis*, II, part 1, fig. 36.
- B. A View of the East Porch from the Northeast. *Ibid.*, I, part 1, fig. 109.
- C. The Southeast Anta and the East Wall of the Cella. *Ibid.*, II, part 1, fig. 25.
- D. Fragments of the Anta Capital. *Ibid.*, fig. 47.
- E. A View of Sardis while the Temple Was Being Excavated. Photograph by Howard Crosby Butler.

PLATE LI. THE TEMPLE OF APOLLO AT DIDYMA—IONIC
- A. A Restoration Showing the Separate Shrine within the Temple Walls. Wiegand, *Achter vorläufiger Bericht über ... Ausgrabungen in Milet und Didyma*, pl. VIII.

LIST OF PLATES

    B. Restored Capital and Entablature. Pontremoli and Houssoullier, *Didymes*, pl. xvi.

    C–E. Sculptured Column Bases from the Main Façade. *Ibid.*, pl. xiv, p. 145, pl. xv. C and E in Situ. D in the Louvre.

    F. The Temple as It Appeared after the French Excavations in 1896. *Ibid.*, pl. v.

PLATE LII. THE TEMPLE OF APOLLO AT DIDYMA

    A. The Entrance to the Antechamber from the Cella. Photograph by A. W. Parsons.

    B. The Cella. Photograph by A. W. Parsons.

PLATE LIII. THE TEMPLE OF ZEUS OLYMPIOS AT ATHENS—CORINTHIAN

    A. A Restoration of a Corner. The Cornice Is Conjectural. *Ath. Mitt.*, vol. xxxxviii (1923), pl. ii.

    B. Details of a Column. Penrose, *The Principles of Athenian Architecture*, pl. 39.

    C. A View of the Temple after Stuart and Revett. About 1753.

PLATE LIV. THE TEMPLE OF ZEUS OLYMPIOS AT ATHENS

    A. A View from the Southeast. Photograph by Walter Hauser.

    B. A View from the Southwest. Photograph by Walter Hauser.

INTRODUCTION

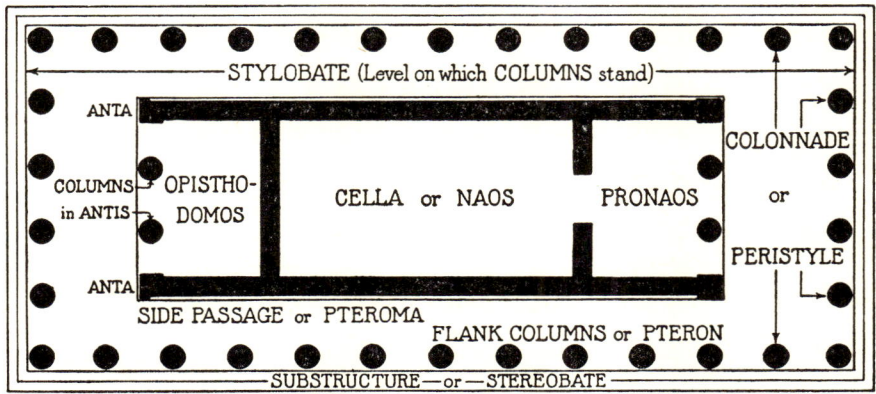

ONE has only to read a few pages of Pausanias's *Description of Greece*, written in the second century A.D., to realize how many Greek temples there were—some in the country, usually commanding a beautiful view of the sea, and many in the towns and cities. They were dedicated mainly to the Olympic gods. Zeus was honored most often, while Athena, Artemis, Apollo, and Asklepios were also very popular. Hera, Dionysos, Aphrodite, Herakles, Demeter, and Poseidon had numerous shrines, but less important deities rarely had whole temples erected in their honor. Certain gods had favorite cities with special abodes there; Zeus, for instance, had his particular shrine at Olympia, while Apollo held sway at Delphi. At Athens Athena had contested with Poseidon for the honor of being the patron deity and had won. But in all these places there were temples to many other gods and often several shrines to the same god in different guises. On the Akropolis at Athens there were temples to the Virgin Athena (Athena Parthenos) and to Athena in the guise of Victory (Athena Nike). Athena also shared a temple with Erechtheus, the Erechtheion, which probably replaced the Old Temple of Athena as the abode of the venerable statue of Athena, Guardian of the City (Athena Polias).

In the case of over a hundred Greek temples enough has survived so that the plans at least can be conjectured. The twenty-five in this book, described in their condition before the second World War, have been chosen for their beauty and distinction. Many about which a good deal is known have been omitted because of lack of space. The Temple of Artemis at Corfu, for example, famous for its pediment, the earliest stone example with sufficient remains to show the design, is only illustrated in the cut on the title page. Of the numerous temples at Selinus, Akragas (Agrigentum), and Poseidonia (Paestum),[1] a single example has been selected in each place. The earliest temple described is the Temple of Apollo at Thermon, dating from the last half of the seventh century B.C. but apparently not the first temple on the site. Remains of other early ones have been found at Sparta, Samos, and elsewhere, proving that Greek monumental architecture had surprisingly early beginnings. The temples are listed as far as possible in chronological order. The dates are, of course, often debatable; many of the temples underwent several changes, or were completely rebuilt, and in these cases the date is that of the earliest fully developed form.

The temple was essentially a simple building (see typical plan on this page), consisting of a central structure surrounded by a colonnade. It was, strictly speaking, the home of the god or goddess to whom it

---

[1] Although Greek names have been used throughout, occasionally the Latin equivalents are also given as being more familiar.

INTRODUCTION

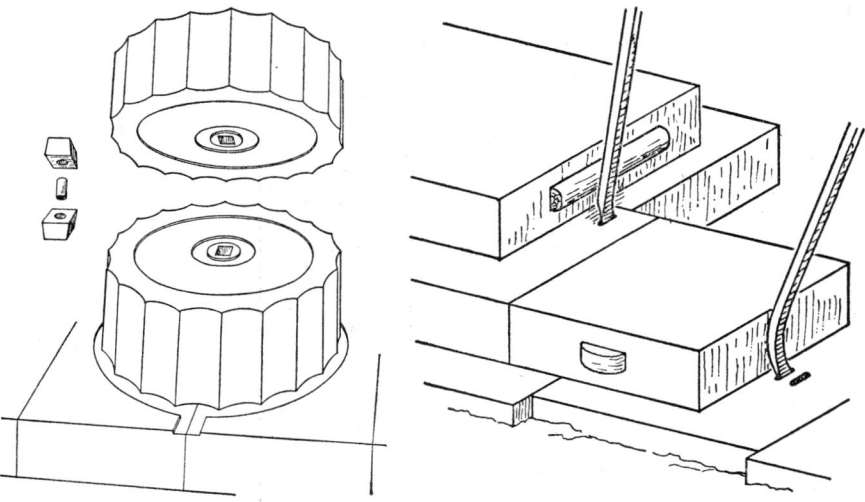

LEFT: METHOD OF FASTENING DRUMS TOGETHER AND PIVOTING INTO POSITION
RIGHT: BLOCKS WITH PRY-HOLES AND LEVERS FOR SLIDING INTO PLACE

was dedicated, not a place for a congregation to worship in, as it usually consisted of no more than the sanctuary and two porches. A few temples were open only once or twice a year. In some the worshipers had to pray to the image from the doorway, in one or two laymen in small groups could worship from a balcony, and in many the cult statue was fenced off by a metal grille. The house of the god was largely furnished with offerings that were dedicated as a prayer or hope for something much desired, in gratitude, or in fulfillment of a vow. Votive objects of all sorts were given for their own value or for what they represented; they stood around the temple, were hung on the walls, or, if unusually valuable, were locked in the pronaos or opisthodomos.[2] The building often became so congested that a corps of officials was kept busy making inventories. Worthless objects were periodically thrown out in heaps near by, and these heaps have now become interesting deposits for excavation. In front of the temple there almost always stood a broad altar, usually with steps for the officiating priest. Here the worshiper made his offering, frequently a burnt one so that the god might delight in the savory smoke.[3]

Temples were usually built on sites already made holy by an altar or by a series of successively larger buildings consisting at first of an altar and an image with a roof over it, then a combination of these or an enlargement of one of them. The early temples are often indistinguishable from the early houses, as at Thermon. From such crude beginnings temple architecture developed rapidly; colonnades were added, grinning Medusa-heads gave way to gaily painted pedimental groups such as those of poros found on the Akropolis at Athens, which in their turn were replaced by marble ones. As temples became larger their cult statues became more monumental and were made of more valuable materials—except those that were incredibly ancient and were said, indeed, to have fallen from heaven.

[2] Technical terms are explained in the Glossary.
[3] Lucian in his *Ikaromenippos* describes such pleasures of the gods.

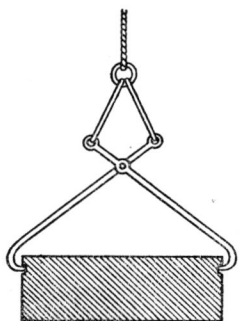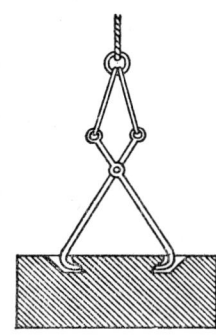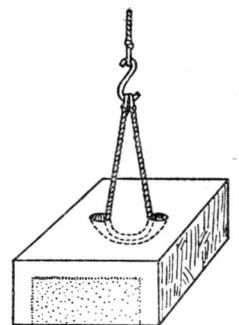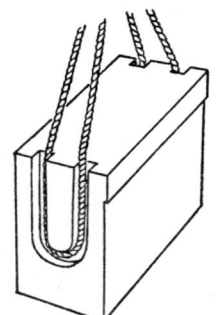

METHODS OF HOISTING BLOCKS: LIFTING TONGS, A LEWIS, AND ROPES PASSED THROUGH CUTTINGS

INTRODUCTION

The beauty of Greek temples was the result of care in planning and precision of workmanship. Perhaps today, with our taste for simplicity, we prefer to imagine some of them less crowded with sculpture, architectural and votive; certainly the sunlight shining through them instead of on them gives a new kind of beauty, a feeling of agelessness, and a rare sense of peace. Whatever else has changed, their lovely framing of mountains and sea is still there.

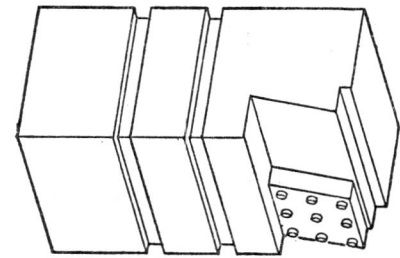

The earliest colonnaded temples were built of sun-baked brick walls with wooden columns and entablature and sometimes a stone dado to keep the brick courses from contact with the moist earth. Later the walls, columns, and eventually the ceilings, were built of stone, the only wooden parts being the roof construction, the door casings, and the doors. The roof tiles, antefixes, and akroteria, which had been of terracotta, were also often made of stone.

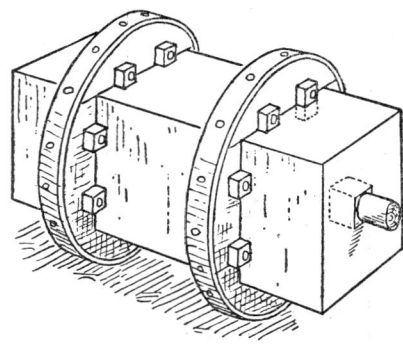

BLOCKS WITH ROPE CUTTINGS FOR HOISTING AND HOOPS FOR ROLLING

These first temples were unnecessarily massive, for the Greeks underrated the strength of stone. Occasionally, as at Akragas and in the Propylaia at Athens, the stone beams were hollowed out for lightness and the hollow partly filled with iron for extra strength.[4] The stone was limestone, poros, or conglomerate, usually coated with stucco to give a richer appearance, or marble. It was quarried locally if possible, to save the expense of transportation (at Delphi the cost of transporting the stone used for the fourth-century Temple of Apollo was ten times the original cost of the stone). In the later sixth century B.C. marble was used for the sculpture, and when the Pentelic quarries were developed in the fifth century B.C. whole temples were built of marble.

Usually the foundations were concentric rectangles, one for the colonnade and one for the cella, but occasionally the temple stood on a solid platform or with each column on its own particular foundation. The walls were built of ashlar masonry without mortar or binding, the dressed edges only of the vertical joints being brought in contact. Blocks were beveled and were extra-long so that surfaces injured in transportation could be chiseled down. Pry-holes and shift-holes helped in the placing of the blocks after they had been hoisted by lewises or tongs, or by ropes in channels cut for them, bosses, and derricks.

Blocks in the same course were fastened by clamps, of which various types are shown below. The first two were used in the sixth and early fifth centuries. The next, the double-T clamp, appeared in some late sixth-century, many fifth-century, and occasionally later buildings. The fourth type, the hook clamp, was the most efficient; it has been found in one or two early buildings but was mostly used in the fourth century

[4] Cf. W. B. Dinsmoor, "Structural Iron in Greek Architecture," *A.J.A.*, XXVI (1922), pp. 148 ff.

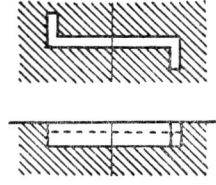 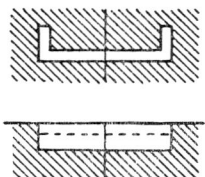 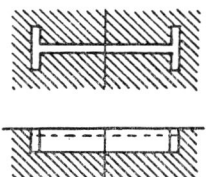 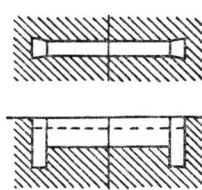 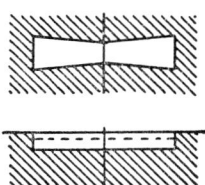

CLAMPS FOR FASTENING STONES TOGETHER

INTRODUCTION

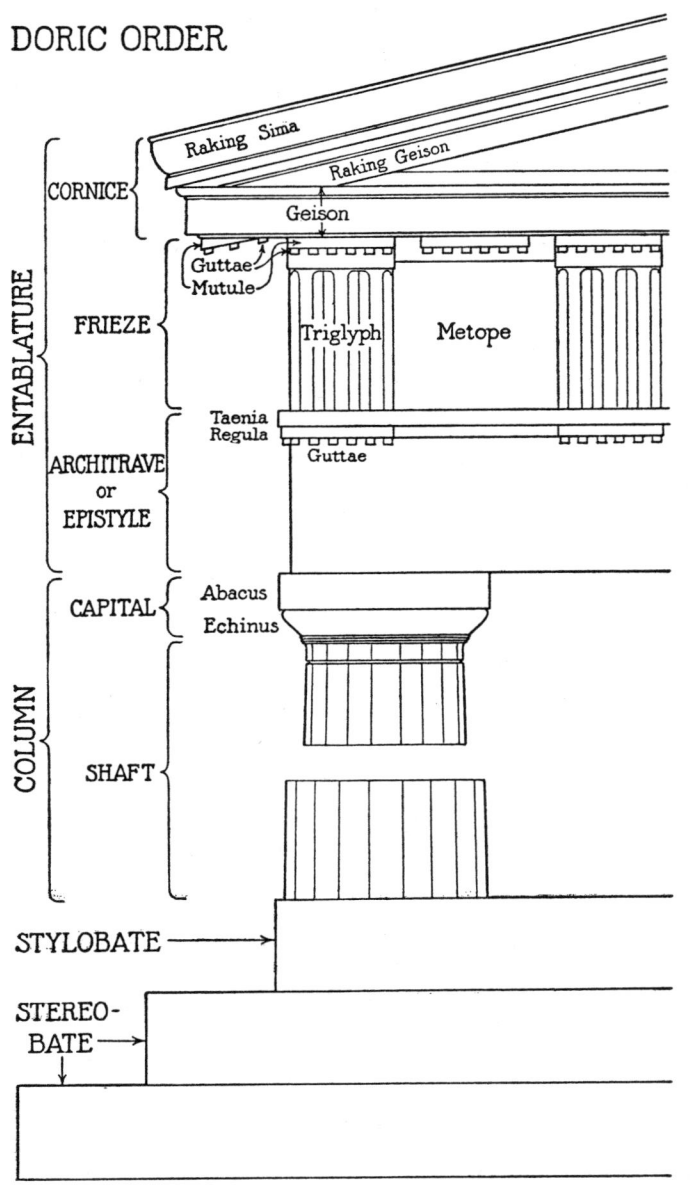

and later. The next, the swallow-tail clamp, had a long history in Greece, covering the sixth to the first century B.C. Iron, or more rarely bronze, dowels secured by lead fastened one course to another.

The columns were monolithic at first but gradually came to be made of several drums fastened together by empolia, or pins, in wooden boxes which allowed each drum to be turned until it settled into a perfect joint with the lower one (see illustration on p. xvi). In later Greek buildings the drums were fastened together with leaded dowels. Only the lowest drum of the column and the necking of the capital were fluted before being put in place; the intervening drums being fluted after the colonnade was erected. Study of the Egesta and Aigina temples has produced the theory that the colonnade was the first part of the temple to be constructed. In the earliest temples the entablature was very heavy, Temple C at Selinus, for instance, having its entablature equal to more than half the height of its columns. In the fifth century the entablature was usually a third of the column height.

The roof construction, except for the tiles and revetments, was always of wood, as far as we can tell. No actual temple roofs remain, although countless roof tiles have survived. The ceilings of both the colonnade and the cella were of wood in the early temples, the former being the first to be made of stone. The old belief that Greek temples were hypaethral, or open to the sky, has been discarded, as most of them show no provision for drainage and their valuable cult statues needed protection from the weather. Exceptions are the Temple of Apollo at Didyma, which had a separate small shrine for its cult statue and in which a conduit has been found; the Temple of Artemis at Ephesos, where a conduit has been found; and perhaps the Temple of Zeus Olympios at Akragas.

The three orders, or styles of building, used by the Greeks were the Doric, the Ionic, and the Corinthian, all embodying the fundamental principle of Greek architecture, the post and lintel system. The Doric and the Ionic were contemporaneous; the Corinthian was a later modification of the Ionic, the only difference being the capital. The Doric order was the simplest, the Corinthian the most ornate. In the early years of their development the Doric and Ionic orders were distinct, but soon, to obtain beauty and variety, architects combined them. An Ionic sculptured frieze softened and enlivened a Doric building, and slender Ionic columns supporting the ceiling gave a lighter effect in the interior than Doric ones in two stories.

Various problems had to be solved in the development of the Doric order as stone replaced wood in

INTRODUCTION

temple construction. The Doric temple was at first too heavy, with the superstructure sometimes as much as half as high as its supporting columns. The echini bulged as if pressed out by the weight above them; the shafts, often monolithic with only sixteen (occasionally twenty) flutes were too sturdy, sometimes measuring in height only four to five times their lower diameters. The triglyphs and metopes were difficult to arrange rhythmically, the problem being how to space them so that a triglyph should fall at each corner and the others should be centered over the columns and the spaces between the columns. (The end of the wooden beam, which the triglyph represented, had of course been supported by a column.) As a solution the corner triglyphs and metopes were broadened, and the intercolumniations at the corner, and sometimes even the second ones, were made narrower than those in the rest of the colonnade. In the Parthenon the heaviness of the Doric style disappeared: the columns had twenty flutes and muscular echini and were five and one half times the lower diameter in height; Ionic moldings and a frieze added further grace, while the widening of the temple gave better cella proportions.

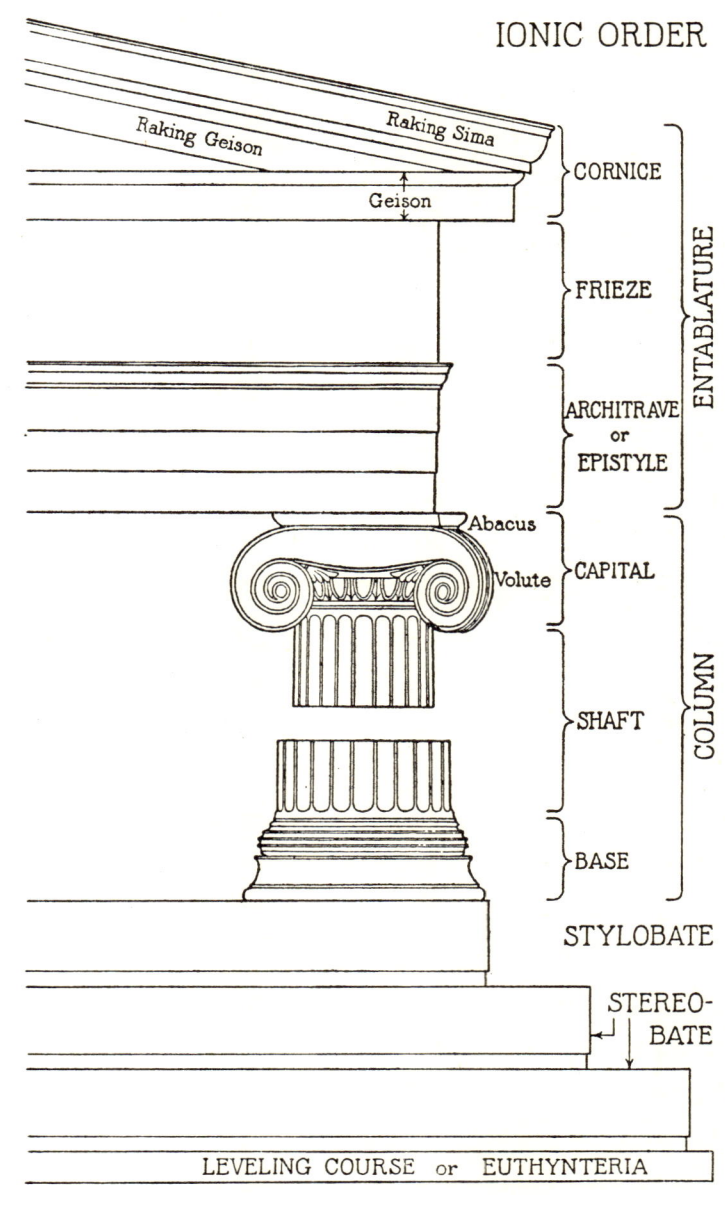

The Ionic order, which developed among the Ionians in Asia Minor, was less massive than the Doric. Above the three-tiered architrave came the cornice with dentils representing the beams of wooden predecessors. Later, especially on the mainland, a sculptured frieze was added between architrave and cornice. This entablature was lighter than the Doric, and the columns were slenderer and were cut into twenty-four instead of sixteen or twenty flutes. The usual column height was eight or nine times the lower diameter.

The capital, at first almost a bracket, developed into a graceful, beautifully carved member, but it always presented a difficulty at the angles of the building. In order that the colonnade should run round the temple always presenting the volutes to the exterior, the design of the corner capital had to be different: the two faces carrying the volutes had to adjoin, as shown in the cross section on the next page, instead of being opposite. The columns rested not directly on the stylobate like the Doric ones, but on bases. These bases were of two types: the Asiatic, which consisted of a torus, or convex member, supported by a disk often fluted into two scotias, or concave members; and the Attic with torus, scotia, and torus—or, in profile, convex, concave, convex. The twenty-four flutes of the shafts were deep and had flat edges, instead of coming to a point as in the Doric.

INTRODUCTION

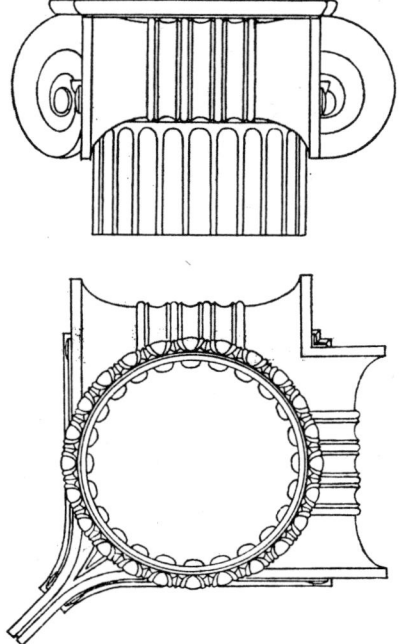

SIDE VIEW AND PLAN OF IONIC CORNER CAPITAL

The Corinthian order added to the Ionic a symmetrical capital, bell-shaped and clothed in acanthus leaves, which could be used without trouble at corners. (For Corinthian capitals see plates XLVIII, B, and LIII, B.) The earliest example (now lost) of this more ornate capital was found at Bassai, where there seem to have been three at the end of the cella (pl. XXVII). The Corinthian order was very popular in Roman times and was widely used by the architects of the Renaissance.

Many theories have arisen of how Greek temples were designed. These vary from arithmetical explanations in terms of the Attic foot, based on the precepts of Vitruvius,[5] to geometrical explanations such as the so-called divine proportion[6] and "dynamic symmetry."[7] The plans of many temples were restricted by their having to occupy sacred sites.

The refinements in Greek temple design are a study in themselves. They are, briefly: in plan, barely perceptible curves, concave to the exterior; in elevation, curves of the stylobate and the entablature, convex in relation to the ground to prevent an apparent sagging of the temple in the middle[8]; entasis, or swelling of the columns, to avoid rigidity; inward inclination of columns to make for compactness and unity and, as a balance and to give variety to the play of light, outward inclination of the small vertical upper surfaces; narrowing of the intercolumniations at the corners to give harmony in the triglyph and metope frieze; and sometimes a thicker corner column to give emphasis.[9]

As a finishing touch to this precision of plan and execution there were sculptured decorations[10] and gay revetments. Color was added mostly in the non-structural parts. The Greeks had discovered that "color upon any sustaining item of an exterior elevation tends to depreciate its appearance of structural strength"[11] and that, conversely, if added to non-structural parts color reduces the impression of weight. The decoration of the interior was also well thought out. We can see provisions for paintings on the walls of the Hephaisteion at Athens, with their stippled surfaces and lead lining at the joints to keep out moisture; but the work of famous mural painters, Polygnotos and others, has disappeared. We have to go to Greek vases or Etruscan tomb paintings to get an idea of this art. Now both color and sculpture have largely disappeared, leaving only the faint weathered outline of a design, or part of a pediment with rare traces of color. In buildings of Pentelic marble nature has added its own color, the iron content of the marble having weathered to a variety of warm tones, from soft yellow to deep brown.

---

[5] W. B. Dinsmoor, "How the Parthenon Was Planned: Modern Theory and Ancient Practice," in *Architecture*, XLVII (June, 1923), pp. 177 ff.; XLVIII (July, 1923), pp. 241 ff.

[6] I. A. Richter, *Rhythmic Form in Art*, London, 1932.

[7] J. Hambidge, *The Parthenon and Other Greek Temples: Their Dynamic Symmetry*, New Haven, 1924.

[8] G. P. Stevens, "Concerning the Curvature of the Steps of the Parthenon," *A.J.A.*, XXXVIII (1934), pp. 533 ff.

[9] On this subject see also W. H. Goodyear, *Greek Refinements* [New Haven, etc.], 1912, and F. C. Penrose, *An Investigation of the Principles of Athenian Architecture* (London, 1888).

[10] See Richter, *Sculpture*, chap. VIII; also Shoe, *Profiles*, pp. 7, 183, for procedure and development in the carving of moldings.

[11] L. V. Solon, "Principles of Architectural Polychromy," *The Architectural Record*, LI (Feb., 1922), p. 100; also his *Polychromy* (New York, 1924).

INTRODUCTION

The culmination of Greek architecture was reached in Athens under Perikles in the fifth century B.C., when the Akropolis was redecorated with a new gateway and several other carefully designed buildings. Civic pride, wealth (Athens was Treasurer of the Confederacy of Delos), and the quarries of Mount Pentelikon near by made this possible. In the fourth century B.C. the most outstanding temple built was the Temple of Artemis at Ephesos, which was one of the Seven Wonders of the World. The sanctuaries of the Hellenistic period show progress in plan and architectural grandeur but lack the earlier refinement of detail and beauty of carving.

GENERAL BOOKS ON GREEK ARCHITECTURE
(A brief bibliography is given under each temple)

ANDERSON, W. J., and SPIERS, R. P., *The Architecture of Ancient Greece*, revised by W. B. Dinsmoor, New York and London, 1927. Contains a selected bibliography.

FOWLER, H. N., and WHEELER, J. R., *A Handbook of Greek Archaeology*, New York, etc., 1909. Chapter on architecture by G. P. Stevens.

ROBERTSON, D. S., *A Handbook of Greek and Roman Architecture*, Cambridge [Eng.], 1929. Contains a detailed bibliography.

WEICKERT, C., *Typen der archaischen Architektur in Griechenland und Kleinasien*, Augsburg, 1929. A thorough survey of the archaic period but without illustrations.

THE TEMPLE OF APOLLO THERMIOS AT THERMON

LAST HALF OF THE VII CENTURY B. C.   PLATES I AND II

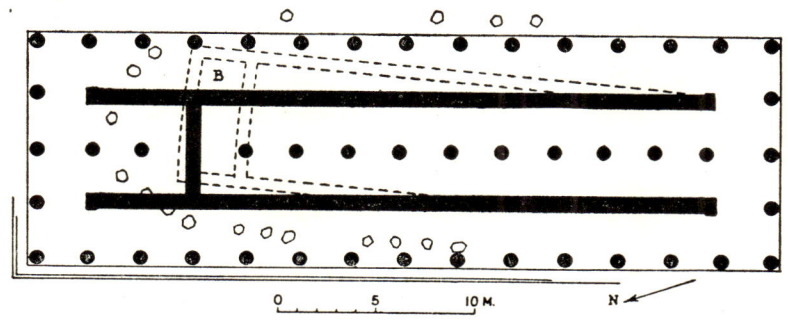

DORIC, PENTASTYLE, WITH FIFTEEN COLUMNS ON THE FLANK
STYLOBATE 39 ft. 10 in. x 125 ft. 5 in. (12.14 m. x 38.23 m.)

IN the mountains of Aitolia, inland in a northerly direction from what is now called the Gulf of Patras, was the important town of Thermon, the scene of the yearly festival of the Aitolian League when its magistrates were chosen. Thermon was ancient; remains of apsidal buildings have been found there, a type of architecture occurring from prehistoric times into the Geometric period (x–viii century). And Thermon was wealthy; its splendid Temple of Apollo was crowded with votive statues. Polybios[1] reports that Philip V of Macedon, raiding the city at the end of the third century, found two thousand to destroy.

The Temple of Apollo, which faced south, not east as was more usual in Greek temples, apparently underwent several different stages of construction. The first building was without a peristyle, rectangular in effect but with slightly curved walls of crude, unburnt brick. Somewhat later thin stone slabs, of which eighteen remain, were arranged in a curve encircling the north end and the two sides to support wooden columns. These columns necessitated a new roof, probably sloping at the north and ending in a pediment at the south. It is not certain whether this building, called Megaron B (see B in the plan), was a temple, a dwelling, or a dwelling used as a temple after the peristyle was added. The original cella has been dated as early as the tenth century B.C. and the peristyle arrangement in the ninth or eighth century.

The succeeding building, dated in the last half of the seventh century, had a slightly different orientation. It had a long, narrow cella with an opisthodomos (or chamber open at the rear) and a single row of interior columns to support the roof. The walls were of brick, and the entablature, the rectangular peristyle, and the interior columns were of wood. Like its remodeled predecessor, it apparently had a roof sloping at the north end and a pediment above the south end, or entrance. At some time in its history a stone colonnade with a continuous foundation replaced the separately supported wooden columns.

The temple seems to have been lavishly decorated with terracottas, particularly with antefixes in the form of human and satyr heads which ran all the way around the roof (pls. I, A and B, and II, E), even up over the pediments. According to tradition Boutades of Sikyon, a terracotta worker in Corinth, was the

---

[1] v.9 and xi.7.

first to make antefixes in this form. We know at least that Corinth had a great terracotta industry and that she exported architectural terracottas, sometimes with directions for setting them up. At Thermon, besides such antefixes, terracotta metopes with mythological subjects vigorously executed and gaily painted in black, white, red, and orange have been recovered (pl. II, A, B, C, and D). They were perhaps made at Thermon by Corinthian artists out of local clay with a slip of Corinthian clay; one has a Corinthian inscription on the back. Numerous other terracottas have been excavated—flat pan-tiles, ridged cover tiles, curved ridge tiles, waterspouts in the form of heads of men and satyrs with female heads to go between them, and an apex akroterion which may have been a gorgon's head. It is not certain which of these revetments belonged to the original building and which were added when the colonnade was rebuilt in stone.

About the second half of the sixth century further alterations in the Temple of Apollo took place, either because the roof needed repairing or because the people of Thermon decided to have two gables instead of one. The metopes were left in place, antefixes supplied on the new gable, and old antefixes replaced where necessary. The replacements seem also to be of Corinthian workmanship but are less striking, particularly the female heads (pl. II, E). New palmette antefixes were placed along the ridgepole, and a new akroterion, perhaps a Nike, was mounted on the gable. Repairs are known to have been made again in the fifth century, for a sphinx and some antefixes of this date have been found.

At the end of the third century B.C. catastrophe overtook the Temple of Apollo, when Philip of Macedon descended upon Thermon and twice devastated the sanctuary. A new temple was hastily erected, with the same narrow plan but a continuous stylobate. As only foundation blocks and poorly carved drums remain, it may not have been completed. The probability is that the temple at Thermon never recovered from the ruinous sacrileges of its Macedonian conqueror.

The temple was first excavated by Sotiriades, who worked there from 1898 to 1908. Since 1912 Rhomaios has been in charge of the site. The architectural terracottas discovered by the former are in the National Museum at Athens; later finds are installed at the Thermon Museum.

REFERENCES

The star * indicates the most important sources for the study of the temple

Dörpfeld, W., "Thermos," *Ath. Mitt.*, XLVII (1922), pp. 43 ff.

*Kawerau, G., and Sotiriades, G., "Der Apollotempel zu Thermos," in *Antike Denkmäler*, vol. II (Berlin, 1908), Text to pls. 49–53 a.

Koch, H., "Studien zu den campanischen Dachterrakotten," *Röm. Mitt.*, XXX (1915), pp. 51 ff.

Payne, H., "On the Thermon Metopes," *B.S.A.*, XXVII (1925–1926), pp. 124 ff.

———, *Necrocorinthia* (Oxford, 1931), chap. XVII.

Poulsen, F., "Thermos," *Studier fra Sprog-og Oldtidsforskning; Udgivne af det Filologisk-historiske Samfund*, 133 (1924).

Rhomaios, K. A., "From Prehistoric Thermos (in Greek)," Δελτίον, I (1915), pp. 225 ff.

———, "Thermos (in Greek)," Δελτίον, VI (1920–1921), p. 168 ff.

*Sotiriades, G., "Excavations in Thermon (in Greek)," Ἀρχαιολογικὴ Ἐφημερίς, III (1900).

Van Buren, E. D., *Greek Fictile Revetments in the Archaic Period* (London, 1926), pp. 64 ff.

Weickert, *Typen*, pp. 7 ff., 50 ff., 142.

THE TEMPLE OF HERA AT OLYMPIA

ABOUT 600 B. C.   PLATES III AND IV

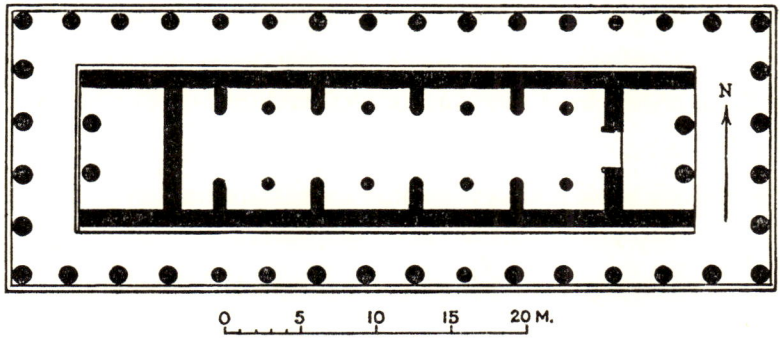

DORIC, HEXASTYLE, WITH SIXTEEN COLUMNS ON THE FLANK
STYLOBATE 61 ft. 7 in. x 164 ft. 1 in. (18.77 m. x 50.01 m.)

WITH the help of Pausanias's description and models such as that in The Metropolitan Museum of Art (pl. XXI, D) one can get a good idea of how Olympia must have looked about A.D. 175, crowded with buildings, both religious and secular, and bristling with statues. But when the Olympic games were inaugurated, according to tradition in 776 B.C., probably only sacred altars marked the site. In the second half of the eighth century a simple temple, without colonnades or peristyle, sacred to Hera and also to Zeus, seems to have been built around one of the altars. Later, when the games grew more and more famous and began to attract contestants from distant places, a new, peripteral temple with wooden columns was erected on the same spot.

About 600 B.C. this temple was rebuilt in the same form. Like its predecessor it had a wooden colonnade, but shortly after the temple was finished the wooden columns began to be replaced by stone members. Such replacements lasted over a long period and may have been dictated by necessity because of warping or wear, by fashion, or by the desire of worshipers to make an impressive donation. The result was a wide variety of styles. The eighteen existing capitals are all different (cf. pl. III, B and C); the number of annulets varies, as do the number of drums, their diameters, the methods of fastening them, and the kind of poros of which they are made. The columns date from the seventh century to Roman times. The intercolumniations and diameters of the façade columns were greater than those of the flank columns; three of the existing columns are monolithic.

The cella walls of the Temple of Hera extended to form the sides of a pronaos and an opisthodomos. They were very thick, at the base made of stone (a conglomerate containing scallop shells) and above constructed of bricks held together by wooden balks. The interior had two rows of eight columns each; the alternate ones were originally connected with the cella walls by short cross-walls, but these were probably removed when stone columns replaced the wooden ones. The opisthodomos is one of the earliest known to us. It was enclosed for use as a treasury and could not be entered from the temple itself. Here, in the time of Pausanias, stood the only remaining wooden column.

A limestone base in the cella belonged to the cult statue. A colossal limestone head of Hera (pl. IV, B) with traces of red was found in the excavations. As it is of very soft stone and is not much weathered, it

THE TEMPLE OF HERA AT OLYMPIA

must have belonged to a statue that stood indoors and was probably the head of the cult statue in the Temple of Hera, the only temple in Olympia before the fifth century. Pausanias tells us that Hera was seated on a throne and beside her stood Zeus, bearded and helmeted.

Early in the fifth century the famous Temple of Zeus was built at Olympia, leaving the Heraion the abode of Hera alone but still a much frequented building, for the cult of the goddess was important because of her association with Zeus. It was through Hera's influence that women (married women were sternly excluded from even watching the great games) had a chance to have Olympic Games of their own. There were contests in her honor, based on the men's games, in which girls and women competed, and great processions to bestow on her the sacred peplos woven by her sixteen officiating matrons and their sixteen assistants.

In the course of time the Temple of Hera was destroyed—by floods, rains, earthquakes, and pillagers. The terracotta roof (pl. III, A) fell in, and the cella walls began to weather away, dissolving into the clay to which we owe the preservation of the justly famous Hermes by Praxiteles, placed in the temple by some worshiper. This statue, of beautifully luminous marble, is unique among Greek originals, for we know from a description by Pausanias[1] that it is the actual work of the famous Greek sculptor. It and the few sculptural remains of the temple are installed in the Olympia Museum. The Temple of Hera was excavated by German archaeologists under Curtius in 1876 and 1877.

[1] v.17.3.

REFERENCES
The star * indicates the most important source for the study of the temple

*CURTIUS, E., and ADLER, F., *Olympia: Die Ergebnisse der von dem deutschen Reich veranstalteten Ausgrabungen*, vol. II, Berlin, 1892.

DÖRPFELD, W., "Olympia," *Ath. Mitt.*, XLVII (1922), pp. 30 ff.

GARDINER, E. N., *Olympia: Its History and Remains*, Oxford, 1925.

HEGE, W., and RODENWALDT, G., *Olympia*, London, 1936.

WEICKERT, *Typen*, pp. 34 ff., 37 ff.

THE TEMPLE OF ARTEMIS AT EPHESOS

ARCHAIC TEMPLE ABOUT 560–430 B.C.

LATER TEMPLE ABOUT 356–334 B.C. PLATES V AND VI

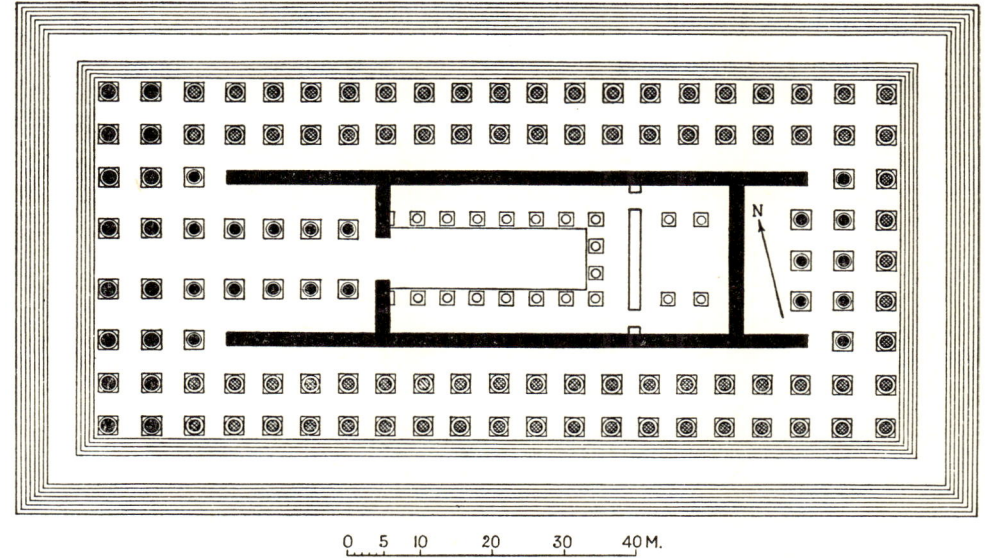

IONIC, OCTOSTYLE (PROBABLY ENNEASTYLE ON THE EASTERN FAÇADE), AND
DIPTERAL, WITH TWENTY-ONE COLUMNS ON THE FLANK
STYLOBATE 169 ft. 3 in. x 365 ft. 10 in. (51.58 m. x 111.50 m.)

THE Temple of Artemis at Ephesos was one of the Seven Wonders of the World. It is said that the goddess herself helped build it,[1] for when the central block of the architrave refused to fall into position and the architect went to bed in a suicidal mood, Artemis appeared to assure him that all would be well. She kept her word and in the morning the huge stone had settled in place by its own weight. Pausanias called the temple the largest building in the world[2]; that it was one of the few Greek temples with the cella open to the sky (hypaethral) is established by the finding of a conduit.

This temple and its predecessors all centered around an earlier shrine to Artemis.[3] There were probably six stages in all in its development, beginning with an altar possibly enclosed by a building,[4] which was enlarged in the seventh century B.C. After two later changes it was apparently redesigned in the time of Kroisos (Croesus) of Lydia. This stage was marked by a temple four times the size of the preceding temple, with coinciding statue base, started about 560 B.C. It is presumably this temple that was said by Pliny to have taken one hundred and twenty years to build.[5] The architects were probably Chersiphron of Knossos and Metagenes, his son.[6]

---

[1] Pliny *Natural History* XXXVI.14.   [2] IV.31.8.

[3] The legend that the Amazons built this sanctuary (Pausanias VII.2.7) points to its non-Greek origin.

[4] See Weickert, *Typen*, pp. 16 ff., 157 ff. Löwy denies the existence of the early stages and thinks that all the earlier substructure under the fourth-century temple belonged to the sixth-century one.

[5] Pliny *loc. cit.*   [6] These architects wrote a treatise on architecture which was later used by Vitruvius.

THE TEMPLE OF ARTEMIS AT EPHESOS

This archaic Temple of Artemis (pl. v, A and B) faced west and was built of marble except for the roof of the colonnade which was, as usual, of wood with terracotta tiles. King Kroisos gave many of its sculptured drums, which, together with its carved parapet, were gaily colored and must have added much to its fame. Bits of sculpture, too fragmentary to restore with certainty, are in the British Museum, together with a reconstructed base with Kroisos's name on it. The column sculptures are about life size and vary in style—a further indication that it took a long time to build the temple. Their subjects seem to be votaries and priestesses in procession (pl. vi, A),[7] as well as warriors and horses. Some of the decorated drums were square and probably stood directly before and inside the pronaos and the opisthodomos. Bulls seem to have been represented on some of these. Fragments of a parapet 0.88 meter high from the edge of the roof were found in the excavations. It had figures, also varying in style, between waterspouts in the form of lion heads, and apparently they represented an assembly of deities, priests, mythological creatures, processions, and combat scenes. Whether or not the parapet surmounted the pediments is unknown.

The final stage of the Temple of Artemis, the justly renowned one, was necessitated in 356 B.C. by the burning of the archaic temple. This catastrophe is said to have happened on the night of the birth of Alexander the Great and was the work of a certain Herostratos, who chose this way of making his name famous. There was a great endowment campaign, and various kings, following the precedent of Kroisos two centuries before, gave sculptured columns. Alexander is said by Strabo to have offered to bear the whole cost of the temple if he might be allowed to inscribe his name on it, but the offer was tactfully refused. The architects seem to have been Demetrios, a priest of Artemis, and Paionios of Ephesos. One of the sculptured drums is said to be by Skopas, and while the Alkestis drum in the British Museum (pl. vi, B) resembles what we know of his style, we cannot be sure that it is his work.

The new temple followed the same plan[8] as the old one and like it faced west. Nine steps led up to the stylobate, for this temple was on a level nine feet higher than the preceding one. Bases and drums of the archaic temple served as fillers for the foundations. It was also hypaethral, but the roof of the peristyle differed from the preceding one in being of marble, and the sima had an acanthus design instead of figures. The position of the sculptured drums, of which Pliny says there were thirty-six,[9] is uncertain. It was formerly thought that the round drums surmounted the square ones (pl. vi, c), but it seems more likely that the square drums were in the pronaos and the opisthodomos, as in the Temple of Artemis at Sardis, which was greatly influenced by the Ephesos temple. Adding a row of round sculptured drums directly before either porch and two complete rows at the front of the temple would account for the thirty-six effectively. The subjects seem to be connected with Artemis, Herakles, and various other deities; but these, like the archaic examples, are fragmentary.[10]

For six hundred years this temple stood, rich with votive offerings, the busy shrine of a flourishing city[11] until, burned and plundered by the Goths about A.D. 262, it fell into ruin and was so thoroughly

---

[7] The Metropolitan Museum has a colored cast of this.

[8] There are 117 columns on the plan instead of the 127 mentioned by Pliny, on the theory that "CXXVII" was a mistake for "CXVII." See W. J. Anderson and R. P. Spiers, *The Architecture of Ancient Greece* (revised by W. B. Dinsmoor; New York and London, 1927), pp.140 ff.

[9] *Op. cit.* XXXVI.14.

[10] See the casts in the Metropolitan Museum.

[11] That the worshipers were ardent, if not always disinterested, can be seen from the Bible, Acts 19. 23–41.

absorbed by the swampy land on which it was built that Wood, who spent six years at Ephesos, had to dig down almost twenty feet before he found the site. In excavating it (from 1869 to 1874) he, and later Hogarth (from 1904 to 1905), both working for the British Museum, struck springs, so that their work was frequently delayed by pumping. After their occupation, nature again claimed the spot and covered their work with swamps and vegetation.

REFERENCES

The star * indicates the most important sources for the study of the temple

*BENNDORF, O., *Forschungen in Ephesos*, Vienna, 1906.

*HOGARTH, D. G., and others, *Excavations at Ephesus: the Archaic Artemisia*, London, 1908.

KRISCHEN, F., "Das Artemesion von Ephesos," *Wilhelm Dörpfeld Festschrift* (Berlin, 1933), pp. 71 ff.

LETHABY, W. R., "The Earlier Temple of Artemis at Ephesos," *J.H.S.*, XXXVII (1917), pp. 1 ff.

LÖWY, E., "Zur Chronologie der frühgriechischen Kunst," *Sitzungsberichte der Akademie der Wissenschaften in Wien* (Philosophisch-historische Klasse), vol. 213 (1932), no. 4.

PRYCE, F. N., *Catalogue of Sculpture in the Department of Greek and Roman Antiquities (British Museum)*, vol. I (London, 1928), part I, pp. 35 ff.

SMITH, A. H., *A Catalogue of Sculpture in the Department of Greek and Roman Antiquities (British Museum)*, vol. II (London, 1900), pp. 165 ff.

*WOOD, J. T., *Discoveries at Ephesus*, London, 1877.

THE TEMPLE OF ATHENA (?) AT ASSOS

ABOUT 540 B. C.   PLATES VII AND VIII

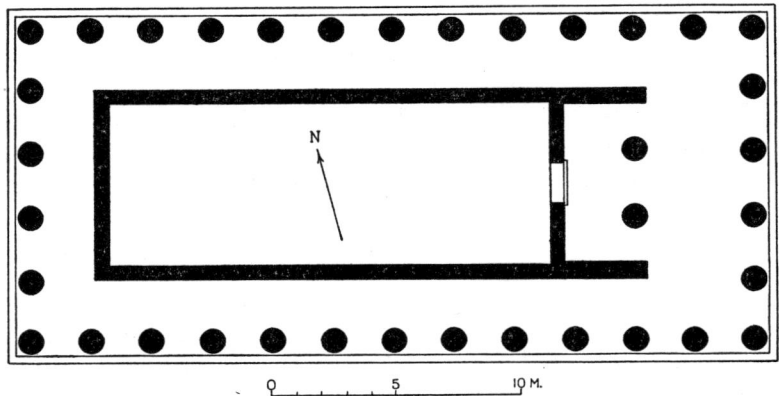

DORIC, HEXASTYLE, WITH THIRTEEN COLUMNS ON THE FLANK
STYLOBATE 46 ft. x 99 ft. 5 in. (14.02 m. x 30.30 m.)

AT Assos, about forty miles from Troy, built on an extinct volcano close by the sea and looking south towards the island of Lesbos, stood a temple believed to have been dedicated to Athena. It was a strangely hybrid building—Doric in spite of being in Asia Minor but with many Ionic touches. The material was a hard, brittle local stone—a form of trachyte called andesite which, when chiseled, breaks off unevenly because of the crystals in its composition. Nevertheless the entire exterior face of the architrave of the temple was sculptured and likewise some of the metopes. We know of no other temple in Greece or Magna Graecia with a carved architrave. This member was usually left plain in accordance with the Greek custom of not decorating the structural parts of buildings. The drawing in plate VII, A shows the success of the decoration in spite of the crudeness of the medium at the sculptors' disposal.

The temple had many irregularities and no refinements in plan or in execution except in the cutting of the stone joints (anathyrosis). It had no opisthodomos; the pronaos was set rather far back from the columns of the façade—on a line with the third column of the side colonnades—and its two columns had eighteen flutes each instead of sixteen as on the peripteral columns. There was a greater space between the two central columns on the eastern façade than elsewhere.

Irregularities can also be seen in the length of the architrave blocks, the width of the metopes and triglyphs, the height of the drums, and even in the echinus profiles. Bosses for use in lifting still remain on some of the blocks, as well as the marks of grapples, lewises, and U-holes for loops of rope (pl. VII, C). Swallowtail clamps have been found, one of which is in the Museum of Fine Arts in Boston. The roof construction was of terracotta with black-glazed pan-tiles and cover tiles. Antefixes in the form of palmettes decorated the sides. Over the pediments, which were shallow and show no traces of sculpture, was a terracotta sima ending at each corner with a lion head of tufa. The akroteria, also of tufa, were in the form of sphinxes or griffins at the sides and volute designs at the ridge. The roof was apparently repaired in the

THE TEMPLE OF ATHENA (?) AT ASSOS

fourth century B.C., as was also the cella floor, which was decorated with a new mosaic at this time (pl. VII, B).

Remains of the sculpture are in the Istanbul Museum, the Louvre, and the Boston Museum.[1] The Istanbul pieces were acquired under the Turkish law which demanded that two thirds of all finds in its own territory go to Turkey. The Louvre pieces were given by a sultan to Louis Philippe, and the Boston examples (see pl. VIII, A and B) represent one third of the finds of the American excavators who dug at Assos from 1881 to 1883.

The reconstruction of the sculptured architrave has therefore been possible on paper only. The exploits of Herakles probably occupied the façades, framed on either side by sphinxes. On the flanks were fighting or heraldic animals. Over the entrance were the combat of Herakles and Triton amid bystanders, a symposium, and an unknown subject (one of the blocks is missing). At the western end Herakles battled with centaurs on Mount Pholoë. Some of the centaurs have human forelegs, an archaic representation causing an uncouth gait, and others are of the later equine type.

The small number of carved metopes found indicates that only those of the façades were decorated. These had various animal and human subjects. The metopes were cut at the edges to fit into grooves at the sides of the triglyphs. A regula, cut at the top of the architrave and with no guttae, stood under each triglyph. The placing of these unevenly spaced regulae under triglyphs of varying sizes helped Sartiaux to determine plausibly the position of the blocks and to reconstruct the design. The temple was apparently not stuccoed, for the color seems to have been applied directly to the stone. Traces of vermilion have been found on the annulets of the capitals.

No ancient traveler has left a description of Assos for us; not until the early nineteenth century do we get a definite picture of the state of the temple. We know that Assos had connections with Attica in the fifth century B.C. and that later Aristotle spent some time at court there. The remains of numerous buildings and a large market place unearthed by the Archaeological Institute of America bear witness to the existence of a busy town. The Temple of Athena was perhaps demolished after the edict of Theodosius I in the fourth century A.D. Byzantine and Turkish pillagers finally reduced it to its foundations.

[1] See also the casts in the Metropolitan Museum.

REFERENCES
The star * indicates the most important source for the study of the temple

CASKEY, L. D., *Catalogue of Greek and Roman Sculpture (Museum of Fine Arts, Boston)* (Cambridge [Mass.], 1925), pp. 10–15.

*CLARKE, J. T., BACON, F. H., and KOLDEWEY, R., *Investigations at Assos*, Cambridge [Mass.], etc., 1902–1921.

MENDEL, G., *Catalogue des sculptures grecques, romaines, et byzantines (Musées impériaux ottomans)* (Constantinople, 1914), vol. II, pp. 1 ff.

SARTIAUX, F., *Les Sculptures et la restauration du temple d'Assos en Troade*, Paris, 1915.

WEICKERT, *Typen*, pp. 156 ff.

THE TEMPLE OF APOLLO AT CORINTH

ABOUT 540 B.C. PLATES IX AND X

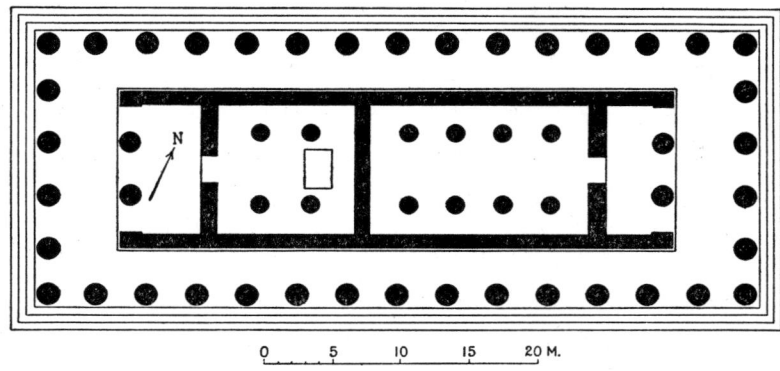

DORIC, HEXASTYLE, WITH FIFTEEN COLUMNS ON THE FLANK
STYLOBATE 70 ft. 7 in. x 176 ft. 7 in. (21.51 m. x 53.82 m.)

CORINTH, one of the largest and wealthiest cities of Greece, attained great power in the seventh century B.C. under her tyrants. She might have gained more fame than Athens had her people not been more interested in pleasure and trade than in statesmanship and organization. She was blessed with a better water supply than Athens and she controlled the narrow isthmus over which commerce on land between northern and southern Greece had to pass. Instead of sailing around the southernmost point of the Peloponnese, ships were often put on rollers and hauled across the isthmus, the Corinthians demanding a toll for the privilege and benefiting by the increased trade. A canal was planned as early as the seventh century B.C., but not until Nero's time was work started on it.[1] Corinth was also a manufacturing town of great fame, and her bronzes, vases, and architectural terracottas frequently formed the cargoes of outgoing boats and pack trains.

Pausanias has left us a picture of Corinth in about A.D. 165,[2] in which, among numerous temples, he briefly mentions one of Apollo. The few remaining columns of an early Doric temple (pl. x, c) were identified from their position as part of this temple by Richardson of the American School of Classical Studies in 1899. It was situated on high land commanding an excellent view of the market place, from which it was reached by steps at its southeastern end. Dörpfeld had excavated on the site in 1886 and made valuable discoveries but had been unable to discover the patron god. As continued excavations by the American School disclosed other landmarks, the identification was finally proved.

The Temple of Apollo was built of limestone and stuccoed. Its columns, of which seven are still standing, are monolithic and have twenty flutes. Those of the façades have a greater diameter and greater intercolumniation than those of the flanks. This arrangement and the echinus profile point to an early date

---

[1] See Frazer, *Pausanias*, vol. III, pp. 6–8.
[2] For a reconstructed description in the IV century B.C., see W. A. Becker, *Charicles*, scene II.

for the temple. It is related in style to the Old Temple of Athena at Athens and the Alkmeonid temple at Delphi and seems to be the earliest of the three (pl. x, A). The foundations, which were concentric rectangles and not a solid structure, were for the most part cut in the uneven surface of the rock and pieced out where necessary. The pronaos was not so deep as the opisthodomos, and into it was built a cemented stone strongbox, perhaps used as a safe for secular wealth, as temple treasures would be in the cella or opisthodomos.

The cella was divided into two unequal parts by a cross-wall. The eastern section had two rows of columns with probably four columns to a row. The western section perhaps had two rows of two columns each and contained a base for a cult statue or treasure chest near the cross-wall. This room seems to have been entered from the opisthodomos and has been considered either an inner sanctuary, or adyton, or a treasury.

It seems probable that Corinth, with her great terracotta industries, decorated this temple with terracotta revetments. A set of such decorations for a large building was found and has been proposed for this temple,[3] but there is no proof. The Romans sometimes used such terracottas as rubble in the foundations of their buildings; consequently few pieces remain intact. None of the entablature has been found except the part of the architrave in situ and scattered bits such as a broken triglyph, fragments of sculptured poros perhaps from the metopes, and some guttae from the cornice. There are a few terracotta tiles with a Roman stamp, which may have belonged to a Roman reconstruction of the roof; the Romans also added a thick coat of coarse stucco to the white coat with which the Greeks had covered the temple. Two fragments of the Pentelic marble threshold of the eastern door—a later repair—have also been found.

Corinth suffered from two earthquakes in ancient times, but what made most difficulty for the excavators was the rebuilding after the Roman destruction. The extensive and remunerative traffic in antiques from ruins and tombs, in which the enterprising Romans indulged, also contributed to the confusion. Twelve columns were standing as late as 1751, when the architect James Stuart visited Corinth and made a drawing of the temple (pl. ix, A). The ruins have been in their present condition, with seven standing columns, since 1795, when five columns were blown up to make room for the enlargement of the Turkish house built within the temple (pl. ix, B). The elaborate building plans of Corinth and the great progress in excavation being made by the American School of Classical Studies can be seen in the drawings in volume I of their official publications. A new museum at Corinth, fireproof and earthquake-proof, has been built to house the finds.

[3] Thallon-Hill and King, *Corinth*, vol. IV, part 1, pp. 19 f.

REFERENCES

The star * indicates the most important sources for the study of the temple

DÖRPFELD, W., "Der Tempel in Corinth," *Ath. Mitt.*, XI (1886), pp. 297 ff.

*FOWLER, H. N., and STILLWELL, R., *Corinth: Results of Excavations Conducted by the American School of Classical Studies at Athens*, vol. I: *Introduction, Topography, Architecture*, Cambridge [Mass.], 1932.

POWELL, B., "The Temple of Apollo at Corinth," *A.J.A.*, IX (1905), pp. 44 ff.

*THALLON-HILL, I., and KING, L. S., *Corinth: Results of Excavations Conducted by the American School of Classical Studies at Athens*, vol. IV, part 1: *Decorated Architectural Terracottas*, Cambridge [Mass.], 1929.

WEICKERT, *Typen*, pp. 113 f.

WEINBERG, S., "On the Date of the Temple of Apollo at Corinth," *Hesperia*, VIII (1939), pp. 191 ff.

THE OLD TEMPLE OF ATHENA AT ATHENS

EARLY TEMPLE FIRST HALF OF THE SIXTH CENTURY B. C.
PEISISTRATID CHANGES ABOUT 527 B. C.   PLATES XI AND XII

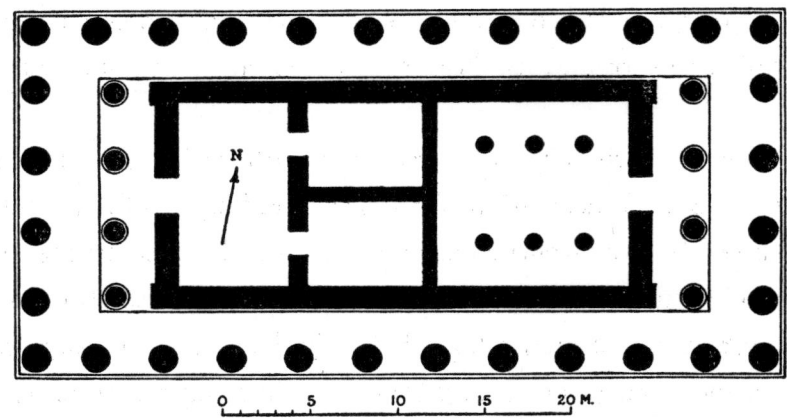

DORIC, HEXASTYLE, WITH TWELVE COLUMNS ON THE FLANK
STYLOBATE 70 ft. x 142 ft. 6 in. (21.34 m. x 43.43 m.)

BETWEEN the Parthenon and the Erechtheion and at one point coinciding with the latter lie the foundations of a building discovered by Dörpfeld in 1885. Its first form, apparently, was a megaron, perhaps the well-built house of Erechtheus mentioned by Homer.[1] The next building on the site (possibly there was an intervening structure) may have been a poros temple measuring about one hundred Attic feet between the pronaos and opisthodomos column centers. Is it, then, the Hekatompedon or Hundred-foot Cella mentioned in fifth-century inscriptions? Did it house the sacred statue of Athena Polias, Guardian of the City, later enshrined in the near-by Erechtheion?[2] Or was it always a secular house (a prytaneion) where the city leaders met?[3] Was it, after its enlargement by the Peisistratids and subsequent partial destruction by the Persians in 479 B.C., known as the Opisthodomos and used solely as a treasury? These and questions about its pedimental decorations are still open to debate.

At any rate, the poros structure may have been built sometime in the first half of the sixth century B.C. Its interior was enough like the Erechtheion to give color to the theory that it was the precursor of that building. It had a cella facing east, perhaps with six interior columns (as shown in the plan), or perhaps four. Here Athena and Erechtheus were probably worshiped, or here, according to the opposing theory, the city leaders met. An opisthodomos and two inner rooms faced west, a most unusual scheme in Greek temples. These rooms served as treasuries or offices. Parts of the superstructure (metopes and simas) were of marble, and several sets of pedimental figures in the Akropolis Museum, of poros, gay with color, have been assigned to this building (pl. XII, B, C, and D). An effective reconstruction of the Herakles and Triton figures and the three-bodied monster, with lions devouring bulls in the center, has been made by Schuch-

---

[1] *Odyssey.* VII.81.   [2] Dinsmoor, *A.J.A.*, XXXVI (1932), pp. 143 ff., 307 ff.   [3] Holland, *A.J.A.*, XLIII (1939), pp. 289 ff.

hardt for the eastern pediment.⁴ At the western end two lions are flanked by serpents. These groups presuppose a colonnade for the building as the gables would otherwise be too small (pl. XI, A and B). A marble sima with a red, black, and yellow lotus design crowns the whole. But these same decorations have been thought to belong to the pre-pre-Parthenon.⁵

The next change in the building was planned by Peisistratos and perhaps executed by his sons about 527 B.C. A stuccoed poros colonnade was added, taller than the previous one—if one existed—and the whole was topped by a marble roof (pl. XI, A and C). The metopes, raking cornice, sima, and pedimental sculptures were also of marble. The latter represented scenes of struggle; on the east gods fought against giants, of which three giants, Athena, and fragments of feet are preserved (pl. XII, A). The remains of the west pediment are scant; there were perhaps lions fighting bulls and other struggling animals. The akroteria may have been Nikai (Victories).

After the Persian destruction in 479 B.C., the temple, if it was a temple, probably was put to secular use. Dinsmoor believes that the sacred statue of Athena Polias, taken from this temple to Salamis before the invasion, was subsequently housed in a temporary shrine north of this building (see p. 46). By the oath of Plataea the Greeks had sworn not to rebuild temples destroyed by the Persians; so the eastern cella was not rebuilt. Blocks from its peristyle and entablature were built into the north wall of the Akropolis, and its western end, repaired, became the state bank and was known as the Opisthodomos. It probably housed the treasury of the Confederacy of Delos. In 404 B.C. the sacred property cared for by the Treasurers of Athena and the Other Gods was placed there. From 385 to 377/376 B.C. the inventories seem to have been irregular. The Treasurers, we are told, lent some of the wealth in their charge to banks, which later failed. To hide the extent of their dishonesty these officials then set fire to the Opisthodomos, and incidentally to the Erechtheion. The sacred objects were thereupon removed from the Opisthodomos, part to the repaired Erechtheion, and part to the Parthenon. The Opisthodomos seems to have been repaired again and to have been under the care of the Treasurer of the Demos but to have ceased to contain objects of value. About 358 B.C. the contents of the Opisthodomos were all removed either to the Parthenon or to the Chalkotheke. Probably the building itself was demolished soon afterward.⁶

⁴ Schuchhardt, *Ath. Mitt.*, LX–LXI (1935–1936), pp. 1 ff.
⁵ Such is Dinsmoor's present opinion. See p. 34, note 2.
⁶ Dinsmoor, *op. cit.*, pp. 325 f.

REFERENCES

The star * indicates the most important sources for the study of the temple

Buschor, E., "Burglöwen," *Ath. Mitt.*, XLVII (1922), pp. 92 ff.; "Die Wendung des Blaubarts," *ibid.*, pp. 106 ff.

Dickins, G., *Catalogue of the Acropolis Museum*, vol. I, Cambridge [Eng.], 1912.

*Dinsmoor, W. B., "The Burning of the Opisthodomos at Athens," *A.J.A.*, XXXVI (1932), pp. 143 ff., 307 ff.

*Dörpfeld, W., "Der alte Athenatempel auf der Akropolis," *Ath. Mitt.*, XI (1886), pp. 337 ff.; XII (1887), pp. 25 ff., 190 ff.; XV (1890), pp. 420 ff.; XXII (1897), pp. 159 ff.

———, "Zu den Bauwerken Athens," *Ath. Mitt.*, XXXVI (1911), pp. 39 ff.

———, "Das Hekatompedon in Athen," *Jahrb.*, XXXIV (1919), pp. 1 ff.; *Antike Denkmäler*, I, pls. 1, 2.

Heberdey, R., *Altattische Porosskulptur*, Vienna, 1919.

Holland, L. B., "The Hall of the Athenian Kings," *A.J.A.*, XLIII (1939), pp. 289 ff.

Schrader, H., "Die Gorgonakrotere," *Jahrb.*, XLIII (1928), pp. 54 ff.

Schuchhardt, W. H., "Die Sima des alten Athenatempels der Akropolis," *Ath. Mitt.*, LX–LXI (1935–1936), pp. 1 ff.

Von Duhn, F., "Brand und Wiederaufbau des alten Burgtempels," *Ath. Mitt.*, XLVI (1921), pp. 70 ff.

*Wiegand, T., and others, *Die archaische Poros-architektur der Akropolis zu Athen*, Cassel and Leipzig, 1904.

THE TEMPLE OF APOLLO AT DELPHI

ARCHAIC TEMPLE, ABOUT 513–506 B. C.
LATER TEMPLE, ABOUT 360–330 B. C.   PLATES XIII AND XIV

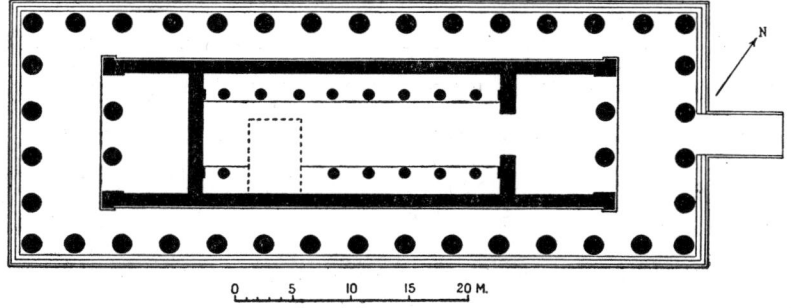

DORIC, HEXASTYLE, WITH FIFTEEN COLUMNS ON THE FLANK
STYLOBATE, 71 ft. 2 in. x 190 ft. 11 in. (21.69 m. x 58.19 m.)

DELPHI, on the side of Mount Parnassos, like Olympia in the Peloponnese, had Panhellenic games for which a truce was declared and arms were discarded. At Delphi, however, the games were eclipsed by the oracle. Here, seemingly isolated in the Phocian mountains yet in touch with every colony of Greece, was the most famous oracle of the ancient world. For centuries, peasants and potentates washed at the fountain of Kastalia, climbed the Sacred Way past the treasuries, and arrived before the Temple of Apollo which housed the oracle[1]; they were met by temple officials, made their sacrifices outside the temple, and drew lots for a turn to consult the priestess.[2] No matter how trivial or how profound the question, the priestess had an answer, which the priests, in turn, were able to put into intelligible form—perhaps ambiguous to give latitude for interpretation. For Apollo, as Founder of Cities, had established a system of representatives in important towns who were most useful to his priests—in executing tithes and keeping them informed so that they could interpret the utterances of the priestess wisely.

According to Pausanias, the Temple of Apollo was built in six different forms during the course of its history. The first was of sacred laurel wood, and the second of birds' feathers and beeswax—unusual, and undoubtedly apocryphal, building materials. The third was of metal—probably a small, bronze-covered shrine which really existed. The fourth was of stone, built by Trophonios and Agamedes and burned to the ground in 548 or 547 B.C. Limestone fragments apparently belonging to this building have been found, but no trace of its foundations remains. It may have been peripteral.

After the destruction of the fourth temple, a great campaign for rebuilding was launched by the Delphic officials. Money poured in—some from as far away as Egypt—and work was started on a limestone building much larger than the preceding one, with a polygonal retaining wall of beautifully fitted blocks. In 513 the Alkmeonids, a noble Athenian family in political exile, undertook this important work, and in their zeal continued the portions already begun in poros, substituting Parian marble, in excess of their contract,

---

[1] There is a model of Delphi in the Metropolitan Museum; see pl. XIII, C.
[2] Euripides in his *Ion* (82 ff.) gives a delightful picture of a youth in the service of Apollo sweeping and decorating the temple and greeting the pilgrims.

THE TEMPLE OF APOLLO AT DELPHI

in building the east columns, the entablature, and the east pediment with its sculptures, as well as parts of the cornice on the flanks.[3]

The limestone parts were covered with stucco, and traces of red visible on the regulae and red and blue on the moldings of the cornice suggest extensive painting. The capitals and columns were like those in the Temple of Apollo at Corinth and the Old Temple of Athena at Athens (pl. x, A). The sculptural decoration can be tentatively reconstructed from the remains now in the Delphi Museum. A quadriga driven by Apollo, probably accompanied by his sister Artemis and his mother Leto, occupied the center of the east pediment, standing figures and fighting animals filled the corners (pl. xiv, A, and B, left and right), and a flying Nike crowned the scene as the apex akroterion (pl. xiv, B, center); these sculptures were all marble. Of the west pediment sculptures—which were of limestone, being less important—only a striding goddess, perhaps Athena, part of a recumbent giant, and some small fragments remain. Apparently, however, the west pediment was full of action, as in the Temple of Zeus at Olympia, while the east pediment was fairly static, composed mostly of vertical lines (pl. xiv, B). About 373 B.C. this magnificent temple was destroyed by earthquake, torrential rains washing down the steep slope, and the settling of the earth around the sacred spring.

Shortly after this disaster the sixth and last temple was begun, and in 305 B.C., except for some fluting and a few details, it was completed and officially opened (see plan and pl. xiii, B). Like its predecessor, it was built partly of stuccoed limestone and partly of marble—this time Pentelic—and paid for with contributions from afar. The architects—Spintharos, Xenodoros, and Agathon—found their plans conditioned entirely by the site of the earlier temple, and the new temple had in consequence some very archaic features: a long, narrow shape and unequal intercolumniations. The cella was poorly designed in relation to the rest of the temple and was broken into by the adyton, really a small building within the temple where the oracle was consulted. The adyton was built, as before, over the sacred spring of Kassotis and contained a statue of Apollo, the omphalos (or navel of the earth, believed in ancient times to be located at Delphi), the tripod on which the priestess sat, and a bench for consultants. A stairway led down into the sacred crypt which contained the spring. The temple was apparently not hypaethral, as no conduit has been found inside; the smoke from the two altars for burnt offering inside the cella was probably let out through a bay or some small opening in the roof. As with many other Greek temples there was a ramp leading up to the entrance to allow processions to move into the temple with uninterrupted dignity. And in front, not on an axis with it, stood the altar of Apollo dedicated by the Chians, which had been there in the time of Herodotos.

Of the embellishments of the sixth temple there are full reports. According to Pausanias, the sculptures in the pediments included Artemis, Leto, Apollo and the Muses, the setting sun, Dionysos and the Thyiades. Praxias the Athenian executed them, and when he died Androsthenes took up the work. There is, however, no trace of these sculptures, probably because they were carried off by the Romans. On the walls were popular maxims, such as "Know thyself" and "Nothing in excess," and the metopes and architrave were studded with shields commemorating victories over barbarians. Paintings by Aristokleides decorated the cella walls, and there were the usual innumerable votive statues and reliefs.

Delphi had long been a sacred place. The Mycenaean earth-goddess, Ge, was worshiped there and had given oracles through dreams before the coming of Apollo. The latter, according to myth,[4] was born at

---

[3] Herodotos v.62.   [4] Hesiod, Hymns to the Delian Apollo and the Pythian Apollo.

THE TEMPLE OF APOLLO AT DELPHI

Delos and after establishing many shrines, came to Delphi, where he slew the Python and supplanted the local gods. Poseidon, however, was given an altar in the temple, and Ge's sanctuary, near by, continued to be used. The character of the early divinity Python was assumed in time by Dionysos, a late-comer, who was allowed to rule Delphi during the three winter months, when Apollo was away. Dionysos's tomb was reputedly the omphalos in the temple sanctuary.

In the early days of the oracle, a Delphian maiden, freeborn and virtuous, was chosen as priestess, or Pythia. But after one priestess had been involved in a scandal, older women, dressed as girls, held the office. The utterances of the Pythia were believed to be inspired by the fumes of the sacred spring Kassotis. As there were no volcanic gases, perhaps when she went below to the crypt she lighted a brazier, which sent a pungent odor up through the omphalos.[5] The priests, whose task it was to interpret her utterances, had obviously to exercise the greatest ingenuity. When Kroisos (Croesus), for example, asked the Pythia whether he should send an army against the Persians, she replied that he would destroy a great empire if he did so. Encouraged by this, he sent his army, but it was his own empire that was destroyed. Whereupon the oracle explained that Kroisos should have asked which empire the prophecy had meant.[6] This episode, and the eventual realization that the oracle could be bribed, shook, but did not destroy, the faith in it. Certainly Apollo's miraculous defense of his temple with earthquake and tempest against the Persians and later against the Gauls was awe-inspiring. Even Parnassos itself came to the aid of Delphi by hurling crags down at the enemy.[7]

In 83 B.C. the temple was ravaged by fire and was restored in A.D. 84 by Domitian (pl. XIII, c). Trajan, Hadrian, and Julian the Apostate extended protection to the temple, but in the fourth century Theodosius I, in the name of Christianity, silenced the oracle for good, and shortly afterward the temple was destroyed. A village gradually grew up on the ruins and remained unmolested until 1892, when it had to be removed by the French excavators. These archaeologists unearthed the foundations of many buildings and reconstructed the Athenian treasury, but today only the views of the deep valley below and the mountains beyond are as they were when Delphi was the center of the world.

---

[5] Holland, "The Mantic Mechanism at Delphi," *A.J.A.*, XXXVII (1933), pp. 201 ff.
[6] Herodotos I. 46 ff.
[7] Herodotos VIII.36–39; Pausanias X.23.1–8.

REFERENCES

The star * indicates the most important sources for the study of the temple

*COURBY, M. F., *Fouilles de Delphes* (École française d'Athènes), vol. II, part 1: *La Terrasse du temple*, Paris, 1927.

*PICARD, C., and DE LA COSTE-MESSELIÈRE, P., *Fouilles de Delphes* (Ecole française d'Athènes), vol. IV, part III: *Art archaïque—Sculptures des temples*, Paris, 1931.

POULSEN, F., *Delphi*, trans. by G. C. Richards, London [1920].
WEICKERT, *Typen*, pp. 44 f., 142 ff.

THE TEMPLE OF APHAIA AT AIGINA

ABOUT 500–490 B. C.   PLATES XV AND XVI

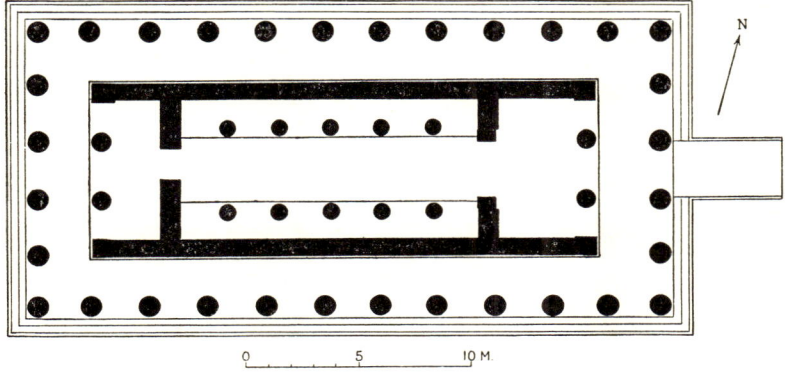

DORIC, HEXASTYLE, WITH TWELVE COLUMNS ON THE FLANK
STYLOBATE 45 ft. 3 in. x 94 ft. 7 in. (13.79 m. x 28.83 m.)

On a hill pleasantly aloof from any of the modern settlements of the island of Aigina, the Temple of Aphaia still stands as a monument to the stirring times when Aigina rivaled its neighbor Athens in art and commerce. This is the only known shrine of Aphaia, an obscure goddess who was an early settler in Aigina, as two temples under the surviving one testify.[1] That she was not more widely known was perhaps due to Aigina's lack of continued political and commercial success.

The identity of the patron deity of this temple was long in doubt. Early visitors thought the temple was the sanctuary of Zeus Panhellenios described by Pausanias, or perhaps a temple to Athena. Furtwängler, who excavated there in 1901, thought it a sanctuary of Herakles, until countless female votive figures were unearthed. He then decided that it was the sanctuary of Aphaia mentioned by Pausanias.[2] This opinion was proved correct when an inscription with Aphaia's name on it was dug up, a fragment at a time.

The temple was fully finished with all refinements except horizontal curvature. The material was local limestone stuccoed, except for the simas and the lowest row of roof tiles, which, like the sculpture, were of marble. No metopes have been found, but these may have been of wood. The exterior colonnade was composed of monolithic shafts, except on the north, where two or three columns were made of drums of various sizes, as were also the interior columns in two stories (pl. xv, A and B). That these three exterior columns were not monolithic is perhaps an argument in favor of the theory, advanced also for the Temple at Egesta, that in Greek building the colonnade was finished first. In this case space would be left for carting materials into the interior. When all was finished there, the three columns would be erected, not of monolithic shafts because there was not room to do this easily, but of smaller drums.

Before the temple was the altar for burnt offerings with a space in front where the Aiginetan maidens probably danced in the ritual to Aphaia, protectress of women. A ramp led from the altar to the temple

---

[1] Welter, *Aigina*, pp. 69 ff.; Weickert, *Typen*, pp. 26 f., 93 ff.; and E. D. Van Buren, *Greek Fictile Revetments in the Archaic Period* (London, 1926), pp. 3 f. See Furtwängler, *Aegina*, pl. 61, for the coloring of the fifth-century temple and its predecessor.
[2] II.30.3.

(pl. xv, B). Walking along this toward the temple, the worshiper would have seen the grille, probably of wood, which enclosed the part of the colonnade in front of the pronaos, making a treasury of it. Above were the pedimental sculptures gaily painted blue and red.[3] Here the Greeks and Herakles fought the Trojans, urged on by Athena, who shook her aegis to terrify the enemy (pl. xv, A). The western pediment was also decorated with a scene from the Trojan war. Athena stood in the center again, this time in a less militant attitude (pl. xvi, A). The apex akroteria were in the form of tall palmettes, flanked by shorter maidens with stiffly yet gracefully falling mantles. Decorative griffins surmounted the corners of the pediments.

There are two sets of figures for the eastern pediment and several theories have been offered to account for them. One, held by Furtwängler,[4] is that, as the result of a contest, the east and west pediment sculptures were the work of two different artists. The extra figures were made by unsuccessful competitors who were perhaps rewarded by having their statues placed near the temple as votive figures. Another[5] is that the second set was a replacement after the east pediment had been partly destroyed by the Persians in 479 B.C. A third[6] dates the temple about 510–500 B.C. and suggests that the eastern end of the temple was wrecked about 487–485 B.C. by the Aiginetan traitor Nikodromos, the pediment being replaced by a new group about 485–480. A fourth[7] supposes that the center of the eastern pediment was shattered by lightning; new figures were put in place in the pediment and the intact old figures were erected near the temple as votive offerings.

A door from the grilled pteroma opened into the pronaos. The cella had columns in two stories and a balcony, like the Temple of Zeus at Olympia. Off center in the cella wall behind the cult statue was a door opening into the opisthodomos, evidently cut as an afterthought. Presumably the priests insisted on an adyton, which was provided by enclosing the opisthodomos with a solid wall below and a grille above. The room thus formed was divided into two parts. In the larger was an offering table, and the smaller one was perhaps a treasury.

Thanks to its isolation, the temple of Aphaia was never made over into a church or plundered to a great extent. Perhaps an earthquake leveled some of it, but more likely peasants looking for metal clamps and the ravages of time effected the final disintegration. When the eastern terrace was cleared to be used as a garden, small fragments were thrown into a cistern and into the ruins of the gateway to the sacred enclosure, where they remained unseen by the French explorers and by Cockerell and Baron Haller. They were finally unearthed by Furtwängler's German expedition in 1901. The many figures found by Cockerell and Baron Haller are now in Munich (pl. xvi, A, B, and c), having been purchased by Ludwig I of Bavaria soon after their discovery. This was in the days when an excavator or his financial backer, armed with a permit, could take home or sell all his finds. These important statues were unfortunately restored so thoroughly with marble additions by Thorwaldsen that they cannot be taken apart for corrections. In the Munich Museum there are also models painted in the color of the originals, based on Furtwängler's study of the figures and the

---

[3] See the casts in the Metropolitan Museum.
[4] *Op. cit.*, pp. 272–274, 353.
[5] P. Wolters, *Führer durch die Glyptothek König Ludwig's I* (Munich, 1935), p. 18.
[6] H. Thiersch, "Äginetische Studien, II," *Nachrichten von der Gesellschaft der Wissenschaften zu Göttingen* (Berlin, 1928), vol. II, pp. 167 ff.
[7] Welter, *op. cit.*, p. 85.

blocks in which they were originally set. They are not entirely correct in detail, but they give a general idea of how these vigorous and effective figures appeared. The finds of Furtwängler during his researches in 1901 were kept in Athens and are now in the National Museum.

REFERENCES

The star * indicates the most important source for the study of the temple

COCKERELL, C. R., *The Temples of Jupiter Panhellenius at Aegina and of Apollo Epicurius at Bassae*, London, 1860.

*FURTWÄNGLER, A., and others, *Aegina: Das Heiligtum der Aphaia*, Munich, 1906.

———, *Beschreibung der Glyptothek König Ludwig's I zu München*, 2nd ed., revised by P. Wolters, Munich, 1910.

WELTER, G., *Aigina*, Berlin, 1938.

THE TEMPLE OF HERA OR THE TEMPLE E-R AT SELINUS

ABOUT THE FIRST QUARTER OF THE V CENTURY B. C. PLATES XVII AND XVIII

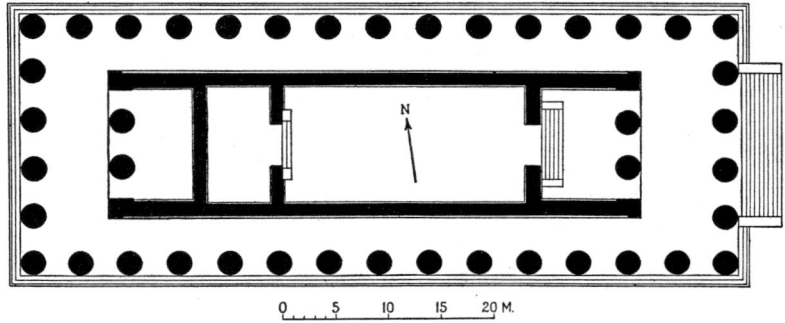

DORIC, HEXASTYLE, WITH FIFTEEN COLUMNS ON THE FLANK
STYLOBATE 83 ft. 1 in. x 222 ft. 3 in. (25.32 m. x 67.74 m.)

AMONG the most beautiful of Greek reliefs are four metopes in the Palermo Museum. The subjects are Herakles fighting an Amazon (pl. XVIII, A), the marriage of Zeus and Hera (pl. XVII, B), Aktaion being devoured by the hounds of Artemis, and Athena fighting a giant. The material is limestone, but, following the tradition that the flesh of women should be represented by white, Parian marble has been inserted for the faces, hands, and feet of the female figures. The contrast between the two kinds of stone was softened by applied color. These metopes belonged to the Temple of Hera at Selinus in Sicily, known as Temple E-R until a dedication to Hera was found in 1865.

Selinus was founded in 628 B.C. by colonists from Megara Hyblaia, a Sicilian town which had been founded by the town of Megara in Greece. It was situated on two hills sloping toward the sea, a thriving city but with no strong natural fortifications. Inside the city walls stood five temples, now a chaotic pile of stones except Temple C, which has been partially reconstructed. On the hill to the east there were three other temples, among them the Temple of Hera. Between the two hills was the harbor and to the west, across the river Selinus, lay a tiny settlement now called Gaggera, where early Greek buildings have been found.

The Temple of Hera was of limestone, stuccoed and gaily colored, without refinements except contraction of the intercolumniations at the corners (pl. XVII, A). Many of the entablature blocks have holes for lewises and U-channels for lifting. The wide metopes of the external frieze were undecorated. The walls of the cella had a frieze of metopes and triglyphs, and the sculptured metopes mentioned above were over the pronaos and opisthodomos. Instead of triglyphs at the corners of the long sides there were tetraglyphs. The crowning member of the cella was probably a simple Doric kymation. Nine steps, instead of a ramp, led up to the grilled pronaos, which, like the opisthodomos, had two columns in antis and served as a treasury. The cella was over 1.30 meters higher than the level of the colonnade and the adyton behind the cella was on a still higher level.

The first excavators at Selinus were two Englishmen, Harris and Angell, who worked in 1822 and 1823.

THE TEMPLE OF HERA OR THE TEMPLE E-R AT SELINUS

They discovered two carved metopes buried in the opisthodomos of the Temple of Hera, but not being allowed to acquire them for the British Museum, left them in situ. In 1824 Hittorff and Zanth, excavated there, and in 1831 several Italians under Serradifalco rediscovered the two metopes already found by Harris and Angell, as well as three others in the pronaos. From 1865 to 1872 Cavallari worked at the temple. He discovered the base of the cult statue in the adyton, which had been altered in Roman times, and a colossal limestone head, which probably belonged to the cult statue. He also unearthed fragments of several more metopes. Since then other Italians have been working at Selinus, but as yet few restorations have been attempted because of the thorough jumble which an earthquake made of these interesting temples.

In 409 B.C., Carthage, formerly a friend of Selinus, sacked the city. It was rebuilt by Hermokrates, a fugitive from Syracuse, only to become subject to Carthage in 405 and to be destroyed again in 250 B.C. by the Carthaginians. An earthquake sometime near the sixth century of our era effectively completed the devastation. Now not even a town remains, the harbors are clogged with sand, and nothing is left of the Temple of Hera but a pile of blocks and drums.

REFERENCES

The star * indicates the most important sources for the study of the temple

BENNDORF, O., *Die Metopen von Selinunt*, Berlin, 1873.
*HULOT, J., and FOUGÈRES, G., *Sélinonte*, Paris, 1910.
*KOLDEWEY, R., and PUCHSTEIN, O., *Die griechischen Tempel in Unteritalien und Sicilien*, Berlin, 1899.

RANDALL-MACIVER, D., *Greek Cities in Italy and Sicily*, Oxford, 1931.

THE TEMPLE OF ZEUS OLYMPIOS AT AKRAGAS (AGRIGENTUM)

ABOUT 500–406 B. C.   PLATES XIX AND XX

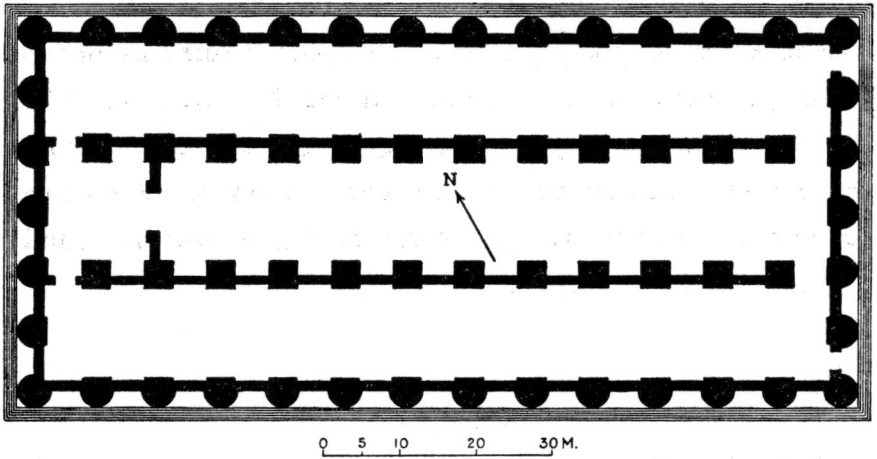

DORIC, HEPTASTYLE, WITH FOURTEEN (ENGAGED) COLUMNS ON THE FLANK
STYLOBATE 173 ft. ½ in. x 361 ft. 2½ in. (52.74 m. x 110.10 m.)

THE city of Akragas in Sicily, named Agrigentum by the Romans, later called Girgenti, and now renamed Agrigento, was famous for its extravagance. Plato said[1] that its citizens "built as if they were going to live forever, and feasted as though they were to die on the morrow." According to Diodoros[2] their luxury reached such a point that during a siege of the city a decree was issued limiting the sleeping equipment of the guards on duty at night to three covers and two pillows. These happy days lasted only from the accession of the tyrant Theron in 488 B.C. to the conquest of the city by Carthage in 406 B.C., but during this period Akragas developed a flourishing trade in wine and olives with North Africa, it competed in the Olympic games, and its fame was sung by Pindar and Simonides.

On a ridge parallel with the sea, halfway between the Akropolis and the harbor, there are remains of a row of temples. Two of them, popularly attributed to Concordia and Hera Lacinia, are fairly well preserved. One, the Temple of Castor and Pollux, is wrongly rebuilt, and one, the Temple of Herakles, has had its colonnade partly re-erected. Another, the Temple of Zeus Olympios, whose site for years was marked by scattered colossal blocks and an enormous fallen giant, has been re-excavated (pl. xx, c).

The Temple of Zeus Olympios was the largest temple in Sicily and bears witness to the fact that the Greeks could build not only beautiful but also unusual and technically difficult temples. The columns were between 14.5 and 15 meters high and had a lower diameter of 4.05 meters. As the local stone was too soft to be used in large blocks or to be lifted with lewises or tongs, the temple was constructed of many courses and the hoisting done by ropes or chains in U-shaped channels cut in the stone. Four items must be conjectural: whether or not the cella was hypaethral, the exact height of the columns, the position of the doors, and the composition of the pedimental sculptures.

[1] Aelian *Variae Historiae* XII.29.   [2] XIII.84.

THE TEMPLE OF ZEUS OLYMPIOS AT AKRAGAS (AGRIGENTUM)

The foundations give the plan. They consist of two concentric rectangles with a filling of rubbish and trodden earth. Five steps lead up to the two-coursed stylobate whose top layer overlaps the lower one (pl. xx, A). In place of a colonnade the columns were engaged in a solid wall which formed the shell of the temple (pl. xix, A). This wall had a socle which formed a base for the columns. The capitals were Doric with a curved echinus composed of two blocks and an abacus made up of three blocks. The entablature was exceedingly heavy and consisted of an architrave three courses high, each with three blocks per intercolumniation, a frieze of monolithic triglyphs, and metopes two courses high. The geison was made up of two courses, and on this was a sima. A coating of white stucco hid the joints and the color of the stone.

Since the distance between the abaci was great (3.35 m.) and the stone was soft, the architrave blocks could not be cut long enough to reach between them. Iron was therefore used for reinforcement, a rare procedure in Greek temples; but even that was not strong enough to carry the entire weight and thrust of the entablature. The final reinforcement devised by the architects was the most striking feature of the temple—a series of Atlantes, or giants, used as supporting figures (pl. xix, B). These Atlantes, 7.65 meters high and composed of twelve courses, were nude male figures, some bearded (pl. xx, B), whose heads and raised arms supported the architrave. Each one probably stood on a horizontal member between two of the columns of the exterior (not inside the temple as was formerly thought).

On the inside of the temple, back to back with the engaged exterior columns, stood pilasters also with a socle forming their bases (pl. xix, A). The actual cella was formed by two rows of twelve piers each, connected by walls. The piers had no bases and were square except for the end ones, which were oblong. At the west end was an opisthodomos, perhaps grilled and probably not communicating with the cella. Although fragments of archaic terracotta pan-tiles and cover tiles have been found, it is not sure whether these were designed to roof the entire temple or merely the space between the cella and the peristyle. No conduit for rain was discovered to show that the temple was hypaethral. The customary large front door was out of the question because a column stood in the exact center (pl. xix, c).[3]

Remains of the raking cornice have been found, as well as a lion head from one end of it. The bits of pedimental sculpture (a head, drapery, legs, feet, etc., small in scale) seem to date not later than 450–440 B.C. and are mostly in the local museum. Diodoros says that the subjects were on the east the battle of gods and giants, and on the west the taking of Troy.[4] According to the same author[5] prisoners from the battle of Himera (480 B.C.) worked on the largest temples at Akragas. Much of the construction of the Temple of Zeus Olympios points to an earlier date, but perhaps the prisoners were available to help with the superstructure and the Atlantes. An altar, as wide as the temple, stood about fifty meters east of it.

If we are to believe Diodoros, the Carthaginian invasion in 406 B.C. kept the temple from having its roof completed. After this date Akragas was subjected to repeated disasters—wars, fires, earthquakes, and pillaging by Romans and Saracens. According to tradition, a large part of the Temple of Zeus Olympios remained standing until 1401, when that fell down. The systematic carting off of blocks to make a harbor in the eighteenth century greatly depleted the remains, but enough is left to give a vivid picture of this once great temple.

In 1802 the temple was studied by Marchese Haus under the auspices of the King of Naples; in 1812

---

[3] Diodoros, however, says the doors were very high and wide (xiii.82).   [4] xiii.82.   [5] xi.25.

THE TEMPLE OF ZEUS OLYMPIOS AT AKRAGAS (AGRIGENTUM)

Cockerell worked there; and in 1823 Hittorff, Zanth, and Stier excavated it. Recent excavations of the site have been carried on by the Italians under Orsi, Marconi, and others.

REFERENCES
The star * indicates the most important sources for the study of the temple

*Koldewey, R., and Puchstein, O., *Die griechischen Tempel in Unteritalien und Sicilien*, Berlin, 1899.

*Marconi, P., *Agrigento*, Florence, 1929.

———, "I telamoni dell' Olimpieion agrigentino," *Bolletino d'arte*, series II, VI (1926–1927), pp. 33 ff.

Pace, B., "Il Tempio di Giove olimpico in Agrigento," *Monumenti antichi dei Lincei*, XXVIII (1922), pp. 173 ff.

Randall-MacIver, D., *Greek Cities in Italy and Sicily*, Oxford, 1931.

THE TEMPLE OF ZEUS AT OLYMPIA

ABOUT 468–460 B. C.   PLATES XXI–XXIV

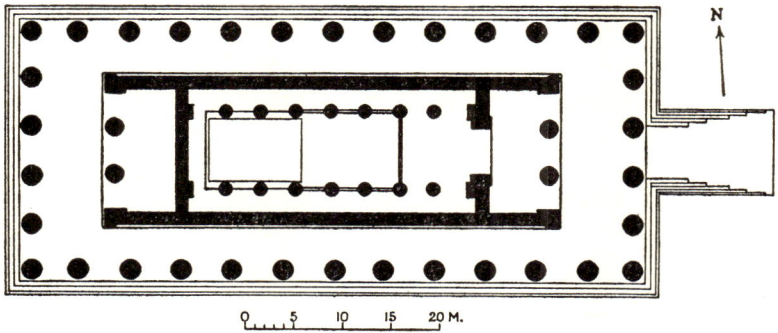

DORIC, HEXASTYLE, WITH THIRTEEN COLUMNS ON THE FLANK
STYLOBATE 90 ft. 10 in. x 210 ft. 4 in. (27.69 m. x 64.11 m.)

OLYMPIA was a sacred place with a fourfold attraction for visitors. It was the seat of Zeus, the Father of the Gods, and the chryselephantine cult statue by Pheidias was one of the Seven Wonders of the World. Olympia had also an oracle. But most important of all were its famous games, held every four years, to which people came from all over the ancient world. The games opened with sacrifices and oaths to Zeus and then were interrupted in the middle for a great procession of priests and athletes to his altar; at the finish there were feasting and further paying of vows to him.

In a commanding position on the sacred way within the Altis, or sacred enclosure, stood the Temple of Zeus, at the time it was built the largest Doric temple in Greece proper—its columns twice as high as those of the Temple of Hera near by (see pp. 3 f.). The architect was Lisbon of Elis, and the cost of construction was covered by the booty obtained in the conquest of Pisa and her vassal states. Unlike many other Greek temples, it was not built on the site of an earlier temple, although the ashes and offerings found underneath its foundations may indicate a pre-existing shrine of some kind. Before its erection Zeus was probably worshiped either in the open air or with Hera in the Heraion.

Models have been made of Olympia, one of which is owned by the Metropolitan Museum (pl. XXI, D), showing the appearance of the Temple of Zeus as Pausanias saw it in the second century A.D. The roof, the sculptures, the decorated sima, and the waterspouts were marble (pls. XXII, A, and XXIV, E), and the rest was of local shell-conglomerate covered with a creamy white stucco. In accordance with the customary practice, the important structural parts of the exterior were left unpainted, but details, such as the lines below the capitals, the taenia of the architrave, the mutules and regulae, the guttae, and the triglyphs, were picked out in color. The backgrounds of the pediments were probably blue and of the sculptured metopes blue or red. The sculpture was, of course, painted and had metal accessories.

The remains of the temple decoration in the local museum are numerous, but unfortunately Pheidias's famous work has survived only in small copies on coins and perhaps in a few late modifications.[1] We hear

---

[1] See Frazer, *Pausanias*, vol. III, pp. 531 f., to which a head in Boston (L. D. Caskey, *Catalogue of Greek and Roman Sculpture, Museum of Fine Arts*, Boston, 1925, no. 25) should be added.

on all sides of the splendor and majesty of this incomparable statue. Dion Chrysostomos[2] said that looking upon it one forgot "all the terrors and hardships that fall to our human lot"; Quintilian[3] said that it "added something to traditional religion"; and Pausanias was deeply impressed by its beauty and the gaily decorated throne.[4] The statue seems to have been put into place after the completion of the temple, for the stones surrounding its base and the black limestone area in front of it were cut to fit the interior columns.[5] It was so large that it had to be forced into the temple and a gallery added to give a perspective of it (pl. XXII, B). Stone screens and metal gates fenced it off, and only the privileged could approach the Father of the Gods in his golden splendor.

Of the other sculptures,[6] the pedimental figures (pl. XXIII, A, B, C, D, and E), probably the work of local artists, were broken and scattered, but their original positions can be calculated from their heights and the unmodeled portions, which were invisible to the spectator. The eastern pediment represented Pelops and Oinomaos coming to make their sacrifice to Zeus before their chariot race, which was to decide whether Pelops should have the fair Hippodameia as his bride (pl. XXI, A). The subject of the western pediment was the contest of Lapiths and Centaurs, in the presence of Apollo, at the wedding feast of Peirithous and Deidameia (pl. XXI, B). The treatment of these pediments is bold and monumental. The two gods are serene and majestic, and the expressions and attitudes of all the figures are well characterized, with the restrained artistry that makes the sculpture of this period so eloquent. Interesting contrast was given to the temple by the quiet, dignified scene over the main entrance and the cleverly interwoven struggle over the opposite end. There were evidently repairs in late Greek or early Roman times, for three figures and the arm of a fourth in the western pediment are of Pentelic marble.

The lion heads used for waterspouts had to be repaired also, for some are late in style and of Pentelic rather than Parian marble. Thirty-nine out of the one hundred and two spouts remain, those of the same date as the temple being of two types. One has an energetically leonine look and a three-tiered mane (pl. XXIV, E); the other has a weaker, less leonine appearance, small eyes, and a four-tiered mane. The akroteria consisted of gilded vases at the corners and originally a dedicated shield on the apex of the eastern pediment. Later two golden victories by Paionios were added as apex akroteria (pl. XXII, B, above).

Six sculptured metopes within the pronaos and six in the opisthodomos represented the labors of Herakles (pl. XXIV). They were full of life and action and, like the western pediment, particularly appropriate to a temple in a city which was the scene of so many contests. Fragments of all have been recovered, the most complete ones being Herakles and Atlas (pl. XXIV, A), Herakles and the Cretan bull, Herakles and the Stymphalian birds (pl. XXIV, D), and Herakles cleansing the Augean stables (pl. XXIV, B). The external metopes were plain stone slabs until the second century B.C., when Mummius fastened twenty-one golden shields to them.

In several respects, such as height of columns and division of cella, the Temple of Zeus resembled the Parthenon. The profile of its capitals was similar to that of the Temple of Aphaia at Aigina, and like the Aigina temple it had stairs leading up to the gallery. The latter feature was probably an addition to the temple after the erection of the cult statue. A ramp led up to the level of the temple floor (pl. XXI, C), and

---

[2] *Orations* XII.51.   [3] *Institutiones oratoriae* XII.10.9.   [4] V.11.1.
[5] There has been much discussion whether it was made before or after the Athena Parthenos; see Richter, *Sculpture*, pp. 220–225.
[6] See the casts in the Metropolitan Museum.

THE TEMPLE OF ZEUS AT OLYMPIA

huge bronze gates guarded the pronaos, which was filled with votive offerings. The opisthodomos was not screened off by a gate but had benches and was used for meetings; it was here that Herodotos read his history,[7] choosing a spot where he could catch the ear of all Greece.

The Temple of Zeus was burned in the fifth century A.D., and earthquakes in the sixth century and the ravages of time practically destroyed all trace of it. The French Expédition Scientifique de Morée spent six weeks excavating there in 1829, and parts of seven metopes and other fragments which they found are now in the Louvre. From 1876 to 1881 the Germans under Curtius excavated very thoroughly at Olympia, uncovering the sculpture which is now in the Olympia Museum.

[7] Lucian *Herodotos*, 1.

REFERENCES
The star * indicates the most important source for the study of the temple

*Curtius, E., and Adler, F., *Olympia: Die Ergebnisse der von dem deutschen Reich veranstalteten Ausgrabungen*, vol. II, Berlin, 1892.

Dinsmoor, W. B., "An Archaeological Earthquake at Olympia," *A.J.A.*, XLV (1941), pp. 399 ff.

Gardiner, E., *Olympia: Its History and Remains*, Oxford, 1925.

Hege, W., and Rodenwaldt, G., *Olympia*, London, 1936.

Smith, J. K., "A Restoration of the Temple of Zeus at Olympia," *Memoirs of the American Academy in Rome*, IV (1924), pp. 153 ff.

THE "TEMPLE OF POSEIDON" AT POSEIDONIA (PAESTUM)

ABOUT 460 B. C.   PLATES XXV AND XXVI

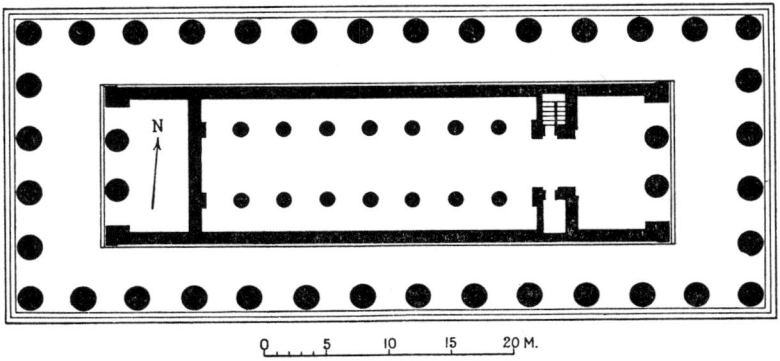

DORIC, HEXASTYLE, WITH FOURTEEN COLUMNS ON THE FLANK
STYLOBATE 79 ft. 7½ in. x 196 ft. 9 in. (24.27 m. x 59.98 m.)

AT Paestum, now Pesto, in southern Italy on the Bay of Salerno, a solitary row of temples basks in the sun. These are the remains of the city of Poseidonia founded by the Greek colony Sybaris about 600 B.C. The site seems less commanding than usual for Greek temples but was apparently chosen for reasons of commerce. Sybaris on the east coast established Poseidonia on the west coast in competition with Cumae, a near-by colony which had useful sister colonies at the Straits of Messina.

For a short time Poseidonia seems to have enjoyed prosperity and fame, as the splendid ruins testify. In order of age, the three temples are the "Basilica" (pl. xxvi, A) with its carved capitals and its single inner row of columns; the "Temple of Demeter," its cella distyle in antis with no opisthodomos; and the "Temple of Poseidon," the largest and best preserved. The names are all conjectures, or indeed misnomers, having merely the sanction of time. The "Basilica" is not a basilica but a temple and may well be the actual Temple of Poseidon, as the earliest temple of a city of Poseidon would probably be dedicated to its patron deity.

The distinctive feature of the latest of these temples, the "Temple of Poseidon," as it now stands, is that part of the upper range of columns in its cella is still in place (pl. xxv, A and B). No other Greek temple has any of its superimposed columns in situ, and few others give such an adequate idea of their original arrangement.

The heavy peripteral columns seem taller because of the unusual number of flutes—twenty-four, whereas sixteen or twenty are the rule in Greek Doric buildings. Their normal intercolumniation on the flanks, is 0.025 meter wider than that of the façades. They incline inwards, with a delicate entasis, and are ornamented with three extra incisions at the necking. There are other refinements in this temple in spite of the roughness and imperfections in the stone of which it is built. There are curves in elevation and, according to Burckhardt, in plan,[1] and there is careful spacing of the end columns to take care of the triglyphs above them.

[1] Dinsmoor doubts this.

THE "TEMPLE OF POSEIDON" AT POSEIDONIA (PAESTUM)

The abaci extend unusually far in front of the lines of the architraves (pl. XXVI, B) and the guttae are long, narrow cylinders. The frieze is two-coursed except at two of the corners, and consequently there is a joint visible across each triglyph and metope. There are no provisions for sculpture in either the metopes or the pediments, but there is some evidence that an apex akroterion was fastened at the western end. The floor of the cella was two courses higher (0.96 m.) than that of the pronaos and opisthodomos, so there must have been steps leading up to the cella from the former. The opisthodomos probably did not communicate with the cella. There are remains of a stairway at the eastern end of the cella which probably led, not to a gallery as at Olympia and Aigina, but to the attic. The altar, to the east of the temple, was about 10.05 meters long by 2.9 meters wide.

Fortune did not smile on Poseidonia, however, and desolation settled down on the town. First its mother colony was conquered by Kroton, and then its steady customers, the Etruscans, were defeated by Syracuse. From 400 B.C. on it was at the mercy of any invader. The Romans called it Paestum and rehabilitated it to some extent, but later the Saracens and other despoilers attacked it. Malaria and the silting up of the harbor further discouraged the growth of the town, and as a result—the only fortunate one—these interesting temples escaped the fate of being turned into quarries for secular buildings. They have lost roofs and cella walls, becoming thereby sunnier spots for the bright lizards that inhabit them.

REFERENCES

The star * indicates the most important source for the study of the temple

*Koldewey, R., and Puchstein, O., *Die griechischen Tempel in Unteritalien und Sicilien*, Berlin, 1899.

Randall-MacIver, D., *Greek Cities in Italy and Sicily*, Oxford, 1931.

THE TEMPLE OF APOLLO EPIKOURIOS AT BASSAI

ABOUT 450–420 B. C.   PLATES XXVII AND XXVIII

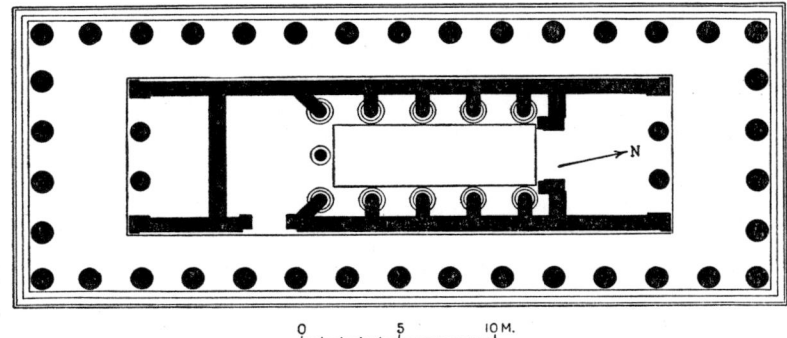

DORIC, HEXASTYLE, WITH FIFTEEN COLUMNS ON THE FLANK
STYLOBATE 47 ft. 7½ in. x 125 ft. 5½ in. (14.48 m. x 38.24 m.)

On a desolate mountain in Arcadia, at a spot near Phigaleia which the ancients called Bassai, stands the solitary Temple of Apollo Epikourios, dedicated to Apollo the Deliverer as a thank offering for relief from plague. It now has few visitors, as it is far off the main tourist routes, being a three hours' ride on horseback by a narrow and often steep path from Andritsena, the comparatively inaccessible town nearest to it. It bears the distinction of being the best-preserved temple in the Peloponnese and of having contained the earliest known Corinthian capitals (pl. XXVII, A). Its frieze, now in the British Museum, although finer in design than execution, is full of spirit and variety.

This temple, on the whole an orthodox one, has several unusual features. Its axis lies north and south owing to its being on a small site made holy by an earlier and smaller temple.[1] A side door led from the peristyle into the adyton, and in the cella, instead of columns in two stories, it had tall, engaged ones, three Corinthian, the others Ionic, and all but one attached to the cella walls by short spur walls (pls. XXVII, A, and XXVIII, A). The frieze ran around the cella on the inside, not on the outside as in the Parthenon, and, like the frieze on the Parthenon, it was "an offering to the god"[2]—the visibility being too poor for the worshiper to enjoy it. The subjects are the battle of the Greeks and Amazons and the combat of the Centaurs and Lapiths (pl. XXVII, C and D).

As Bassai was a comparatively small and poor sanctuary, the temple was built of local flinty limestone except for the sima (pl. XXVII, B), the antefixes, the roof tiles, the guttae,[3] the ceiling coffers of the peristyle fronts and porches, the capitals of the interior columns, and the sculptural details, which are of white marble. Traces remain of the pedimental sculpture and akroteria, but the ornaments themselves have disappeared; probably Augustus carried them off to Rome. Three statues of Niobids, which, because of

---

[1] Weickert, Typen, pp. 29 f.   [2] Dinsmoor, Met. Mus. Studies, IV (1933), part II, p. 213.
[3] See the guttae and molding from this temple in The Metropolitan Museum of Art.

THE TEMPLE OF APOLLO EPIKOURIOS AT BASSAI

material, style, thinness, and subject matter, might fit the pediment, have been assigned to this temple. Two are in Copenhagen and one is in Rome. Some of the roof tiles had openings to let in the light, which, together with the existence of the side door, led early travelers to class the temple as hypaethral. This was probably not the case, however, nor did the cult statue stand in the adyton as shown in the old restoration[4] by Cockerell (pl. XXVIII, B). The first cult statue, a bronze image of Apollo twelve feet high, had been moved to Megalopolis before the time of Pausanias.[5] It and its successor, an akrolithic one, probably stood in the cella facing the main entrance, while the adyton may have served for an oracle or for the use of the priests as at Aigina. Both cella and adyton had wooden ceilings.

The pronaos and opisthodomos were unusually deep, the former especially so, and above them were sculptured metopes. The narrowness of the cella, the fact that the columns on the front are larger than the rest of the peristyle, and the three incisions separating the columns from their capitals all indicate an early date for this temple. The suggestion has been made by Dinsmoor that perhaps Iktinos, the architect, came to the Peloponnese with Pheidias (with whom he afterwards executed the Parthenon), and while Pheidias worked on the cult statue for the Temple of Zeus at Olympia, Iktinos designed the temple at Bassai. The Peloponnesian War, however, seems to have interrupted the work, for some of the moldings and the frieze and metope sculpture are later in style, and date perhaps from about 421 or 420 B.C., after the peace of Nikias.[6]

The Temple of Apollo was destroyed by earthquakes. Its remoteness and inaccessibility caused it to remain undiscovered until 1765, when it was found by a French architect, Bocher, who was later killed by bandits. In 1811 it was visited by Haller, Cockerell, and others. The next year it was excavated by Haller to the tune of native music, and the sculptures were sold at auction to the British Museum in 1814. An English expedition paid a brief visit to Bassai in 1820, and a French one spent three foggy days there in 1829. From 1902 to 1908 the Greeks re-excavated the temple, making some partial reconstructions of the walls and half columns. The capitals and ornaments had either been taken away, looted, or too much destroyed to be reconstructed. Enough is left in situ, however, to warrant Pausanias's admiration for the building.[7]

---

[4] Cockerell, C. R., *The Temples at Aegina and Bassae*, p. 59. See Dinsmoor, *op. cit.*, pp. 204 ff., for other mistakes in this drawing. There were probably three Corinthian capitals.

[5] VIII.41.9.

[6] See Shoe, *Profiles*, Text, pp. 7, 70, 121.

[7] VIII.41.8.

REFERENCES

The star * indicates the most important sources for the study of the temple

*Cockerell, C. R., *The Temples of Jupiter Panhellenius at Aegina and of Apollo Epicurius at Bassae*, London, 1880.

*Dinsmoor, W. B., "The Temple of Apollo at Bassae," *Metropolitan Museum Studies*, IV (New York, 1933), part II, pp. 204 ff.

———, "Lost Pedimental Sculptures of Bassae," *A.J.A.*, XLIII (1939), pp. 27 ff.

Gütschow, M., "Untersuchungen zum korinthischen Kapitell, I," *Jahrb.*, XXXVI (1921), pp. 44 ff.

Lethaby, W. R., *Greek Buildings Represented by Fragments in the British Museum*, London, 1908.

Rhomaios, K. A., "The Capitals of the Inner Columns of the Temple at Bassai (in Greek)," Ἀρχαιολογικὴ Ἐφημερίς, (1914), pp. 57 ff.

Smith, A. H., *A Catalogue of Sculpture in the Department of Greek and Roman Antiquities (British Museum)*, vol. I (London, 1892), pp. 270 ff.

THE TEMPLE OF HEPHAISTOS AT ATHENS

(FORMERLY CALLED THE THESEION)

ABOUT 449–444 B. C.   PLATES XXIX AND XXX

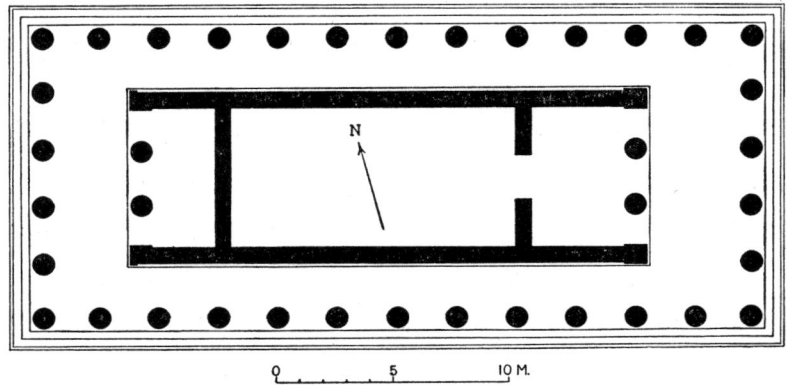

DORIC, HEXASTYLE, WITH THIRTEEN COLUMNS ON THE FLANK
STYLOBATE 44 ft. 11½ in. x 104 ft. 3 in. (13.71 m. x 31.77 m.)

To the northwest of the Akropolis at Athens, on a low hill above the Agora, or market place, is the Temple of Hephaistos, the best preserved of Greek temples externally (pl. xxx, B). From this stalwart building one can look up at the Akropolis and down on the newly excavated Agora and picture Athens in her prime, no longer confined to the Akropolis for reasons of defense, as in prehistoric times, but dotting the near-by hills and valleys with religious and secular buildings.

For a long time this building was thought to be a temple to Theseus, but because of its position and the subject of its frieze it has now been identified as the Temple of Hephaistos mentioned by Pausanias.[1] The frieze, which is still in situ, extends across both ends of the cella above the porches (pl. xxix, A). Over the pronaos it stretches across the pteron to the colonnade and represents battle scenes witnessed by gods (pl. xxix, D); on the west Lapiths struggle with Centaurs. The vanished pedimental sculptures left enough traces of fastenings to be thought to represent the birth of Erichthonios on the east and Hephaistos kneeling before Thetis and Eurynome on the west. Eighteen of the metopes are sculptured, and of these ten showing the labors of Herakles (pl. xxix, B) decorate the eastern end while four adjoining ones on either flank represent the exploits of Theseus (pl. xxix, c).[2]

The temple is made of Pentelic marble except for the sculptures, which are of Parian marble, and the foundations, which are of limestone. The pronaos was deeper than the opisthodomos. Any refinements are difficult to determine owing to the shifting of the drums by an earthquake, but the architrave seems to curve. Vestiges of color, more numerous in this temple than in any other, have given important evidence for the coloring of Greek temples: the carved metopes had red backgrounds, the triglyphs were blue, and

---

[1] I.14.6. See H. A. Thompson, "Buildings on the West Side of the Agora," *Hesperia*, VI (1937), p. 65.
[2] See the casts in The Metropolitan Museum of Art.

the frieze background blue. The flesh of the figures was colored and their garments were mostly red, one being lined with green. The beams above the frieze were red and the coffers had gold stars on a blue ground.

The walls of the cella were carefully prepared for murals, which were apparently never executed. The cult images were probably the famous bronze statue of Hephaistos by Alkamenes, described by Cicero as a "standing figure, draped, which displays a slight lameness, though not enough to be unsightly,"[3] and the companion figure of Athena Hephaisteia made in 421-415 B.C. In the early third century B.C. the sanctuary was apparently enclosed, running water was added, and a carefully designed garden was planted around three sides of the temple. This garden seems to have been elaborated in the late first century B.C., as large flower pots, apparently of Roman manufacture, have been unearthed.[4]

The comparatively slender columns and heavy entablature make the proportions of this temple less satisfactory than those of the Parthenon (pl. XXX, B). Its date has been much debated, but recent discoveries of sherds near it have established the early date argued by several archaeologists.[5] The frieze at the west was perhaps influenced by the Parthenon metopes.[6]

This temple owes its good condition to its situation. The Christians transformed it into the Church of St. George, but although the east cella wall and the columns of the pronaos were removed and the roof replaced by a barrel vault, the frieze was preserved even over the eastern end, where an apse was built. Many of the pteroma and porch ceiling frames and the coffers which fit into them remain. The Christians also cut a large door at the western end, which they later sealed and replaced by small ones at the sides. Tradition says this was a manoeuver to keep out the Turks, who liked to ride horses into the building while services were being held. Sundry buildings for a monastery were built near by from the tenth to the twelfth century A.D., and people were buried there in various periods, but fortunately the Temple of Hephaistos was outside Athens proper under Turkish rule, and so it was not made into a mosque, nor was it within range of the Venetian bombs in 1687. A cornfield grew up around it, an earthquake dislodged a few of its drums, lightning struck one corner, and its sculptures and small south door were used as targets in shooting practice. But such misfortunes and comparatively minor injuries did not cause much disintegration. Now that the Agora beyond it has been brought to light, the temple emerges as the busy shrine of the metalworkers and many other artisans working near by.

---

[3] *De natura deorum* 1.30.

[4] D. B. Thompson, "The Garden of Hephaistos," *Hesperia*, VI (1937), pp. 396 ff.

[5] See H. Koch, *Arch. Anz.*, XLIII (1928), p. 721, and Shoe, *Profiles*, pp. 87, 108.

[6] E. Kjellberg, *Studien zu den attischen Reliefs des V Jahrhunderts v. Chr.* (Upsala, 1926), p. 82.

REFERENCES

The star * indicates the most important sources for the study of the temple

BATES, W. N., "Notes on the 'Theseum' at Athens," *A.J.A.*, V (1901), pp. 37 ff.

DINSMOOR, W. B., "The Temple of Ares at Athens," *Hesperia*, IX (1940), pp. 1 ff.

*———, *Observations on the Hephaisteion*, *Hesperia*, suppl. V (1941).

FRAZER, *Pausanias*, vol. II, pp. 145 ff.

*KOCH, H., *Arch. Anz.*, XLIII (1928), pp. 706 ff. (summary of his talk at the Winckelmannsfest).

LETHABY, W. R., *Greek Buildings Represented by Fragments in the British Museum*, London, 1908.

*SAUER, B., *Das sogenannte Thesion und sein plastischer Schmuck*. Leipzig, 1899.

THOMPSON, D. B., "The Garden of Hephaistos," *Hesperia*, VI (1937), pp. 396 ff.

*THOMPSON, H. A., "Buildings on the West Side of the Agora," *Hesperia*, VI (1937), pp. 1 ff.

THE PARTHENON AT ATHENS

447–432 B. C.   PLATES XXXI–XXXIV

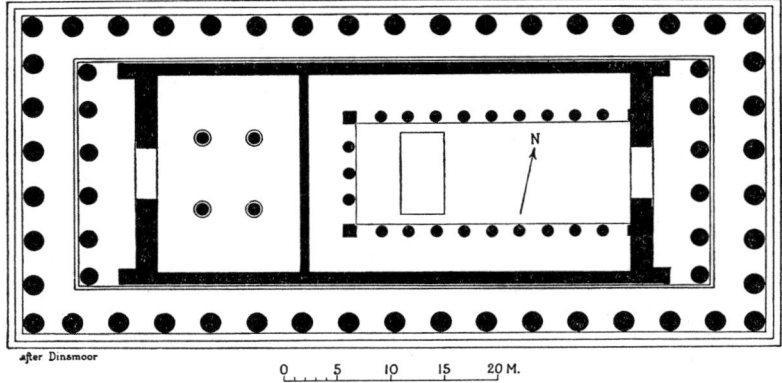

DORIC, OCTOSTYLE, CELLA AMPHIPROSTYLE, WITH SEVENTEEN COLUMNS ON THE FLANK
STYLOBATE 101 ft. 3½ in. x 228 ft. (30.88 m. x 69.50 m.)

THE Parthenon, deservedly the most famous of Greek temples (pl. XXXII, A), is almost too well known to need description. No other Doric temple had such complete and beautiful sculptural decoration; no other temple was so happily planned and so beautifully executed. A combination of circumstances made this building the success that it turned out to be: Greece had come safely through the Persian peril, and Athens had at her disposal considerable wealth, a genius—Pheidias—to direct the sculptors, and a magnificent site on the Akropolis.[1]

One previous building on the site is known; before that we enter into speculation.[2] The pre-Parthenon was perhaps started in 488 B.C.,[3] as a memorial for the victory of Marathon. A poros foundation was built to piece out the slope of the hill, and on this a marble hexastyle building with sixteen columns on the flank was begun under the auspices of Themistokles and Aristeides.[4] In 479, before the colonnade had risen beyond the second drum, the Persians returned and ravaged the Akropolis. The temple was burned, its own scaffolding serving as kindling. Fortifications being considered the next imperative need, some of the charred, unfluted drums were used in building the north wall of the Akropolis, where they would constantly remind the people of Athens of the Persian devastation. There were still many blocks left which expense of transport and economy of material prompted Perikles to re-use when he began his program of beautifying the Akropolis. Drums were used with some paring down, and stylobate blocks were pressed into service even though the original clamp holes were once, at any rate, exposed to view.

Iktinos, assisted by Kallikrates, was the architect who was able to adapt this and new material to the

---

[1] The casts and models of the Parthenon and the Akropolis in the Metropolitan Museum, as well as the photographs by Walter Hege in Hege and Rodenwaldt, *Die Akropolis* (Berlin, 1930), are useful in studying this temple.

[2] See Weickert, *Typen*, pp. 19 ff. Dinsmoor believes that the cult of Athena Parthenos was continuous on the site and suggests a pre-pre-Parthenon decorated with the sima and sculptures assigned by Schuchhardt to the Old Temple of Athena.

[3] For the arguments about the date, see Dinsmoor, "The Date of the Older Parthenon," *A.J.A.*, XXXVII (1934), pp. 408 ff. See also B. H. Hill, "The Older Parthenon," *A.J.A.*, XVI (1912), pp. 535 ff.

[4] It was probably this building which started the extensive use of the Pentelic quarries. Dinsmoor, *op. cit.*, p. 447.

superb proportions of the Parthenon. A large building record inscribed on all four sides with a description of the receipts, expenses, and work accomplished has been pieced together out of bits found on the Akropolis and identified from time to time.[5] From it we know that work on the temple was begun in 447/446 B.C. and ended in 433/432 when the sculptures were completed and the accounts closed.

The whole building was of Pentelic marble[6] except the roof beams and rafters, which were of wood. The pronaos was grilled in with bronze or iron so that treasures could be kept there. The cella, called the Hekatompedos Naos, held the famous chryselephantine statue by Pheidias, dedicated in 438 B.C., which was the cause of so much covetousness and scandal in its day.[7] It was a figure of Athena, about forty feet high including the base. She stood erect, dressed in a long tunic, an elaborate helmet, and her aegis, or goatskin. In one hand she held a spear, in the other a statuette of Victory, and at her feet rested a shield of intricate design. The whole was enclosed by a grating to keep the worshipers at a respectful distance. From the descriptions of the statue by ancient writers several copies have been identified (pl. XXXI, D).[8]

Behind the cella, but not communicating with it, was a room used as a treasury and called the Parthenon, or chamber of the virgin, a name the temple as a whole apparently did not acquire until the time of Demosthenes in the late fourth century. Four tall Ionic columns served as supports in this room instead of the Doric ones in two stories used in the larger cella. The opisthodomos was enclosed by a grille, as was the pronaos.

The proportions and refinements of the building were most carefully worked out to give vitality and play of light. Perpendicular faces are the exception, not the rule: the stylobate and architrave curve upward and the walls of the cella lean inward; the outside columns also lean inward, have entasis, and are as deeply fluted at the tops as below to give shadows; above them the abaci and faces of the cornice lean out. The moldings are few and simple, and the antefixes are so restrained that they seem to belong to an earlier date (pl. XXXI, B). Four lion heads, one at either end of the long sides, are false waterspouts. There are several Ionic details[9]—the capitals in the west room, the frieze, and the Lesbian kymation above it, the carved decoration of the anta capitals, and the astragal over the triglyphs.

The metopes were carved on the ground, perhaps in Pheidias's workshop. They have been dated from about 447 to 443 B.C. because of their style and because they had to be in place before the cornice. The subjects, Lapiths fighting Centaurs, gods fighting giants, Greeks fighting Amazons, and other mythical scenes, were made to fit with great skill and variety into their blocks (pl. XXXIII, E and F).[10]

The frieze, which extended around the outside of the cella wall (pl. XXXII, B) and its porches, is so familiar that its beauty and smoothness of motion do not need reviewing. It is no mere decorative facing but a structural part of the building, for it was carved in situ on blocks twenty inches thick. The carving, which is slightly deeper at the top so that the figures stand out when seen from below, may have been done

---

[5] See Dinsmoor, "Attic Building Accounts," *A.J.A.*, XVII (1913), pp. 53 ff.; XXV (1921), pp. 233 ff.
[6] In the Metropolitan Museum there is a fragment of one of the Parthenon columns.
[7] Plutarch *Life of Perikles* XXXI.2–4.
[8] See Richter, *Sculpture*, pp. 215 ff., and Dinsmoor, "The Repair of the Athena Parthenos," *A.J.A.*, XXXVIII (1934), pp. 103 f.
[9] Kallikrates was probably responsible for the Ionic parts, cf. his work on the Temple of Athena Nike. Iktinos did not have his help at Bassai, hence the Ionic features there are inferior to the Ionic parts of the Parthenon. Apparently the older Parthenon showed Ionic influence. See also Shoe, *Profiles*, Text, p. 148.
[10] For the metopes see C. Praschniker, *Parthenonstudien*, Augsburg and Vienna, 1928.

by various workmen from a sketch by Pheidias. It represents the Panathenaic procession (pl. xxxiv) flowing along to its climax—the presentation of Athena's peplos to her priest, with the gods as invited guests. The assembly of deities is placed over the eastern door (pl. xxxiv, A) and reminds us of the schemes in the Temple of Hephaistos, the Temple of Athena Nike, and the Erechtheion. The frieze has been dated from 443 to 438 B.C. for stylistic reasons and because we know from the records that wood probably used for its scaffolding was purchased in 444/443 and sold in 438.

Work on the pediments was begun in 438 B.C.[11] The figures were carved on the ground and fastened in place with dowels and clamps after the bed of the cornice had been hollowed out or roughed up to make them fit securely. The eastern end represented the birth of Athena (pl. xxxi, A, upper). On the west Athena and Poseidon in the center contested for the supremacy of Athens while various legendary figures looked on (pl. xxxi, A, lower). The remains in the British Museum, as well as the few figures in situ and the drawings of early travelers, give an idea of the beauty of these pediments (pl. xxxiii, A, B, C, and D). There were the usual metal accessories and the usual gay colors tying the sculptured parts together. Acanthus stems with volutes ending in palmettes formed the apex akroteria, which were about nine feet high. Apparently they were not alike; one may have had a Panathenaic amphora at either side.[12]

The vicissitudes of the Parthenon were many. In 334 B.C. Alexander the Great fastened twenty-six shields on the architrave in celebration of the victory of Granicus. In 304/303, Demetrios Poliorketes, who had already been honored by having his portrait and that of his father woven into the sacred peplos,[13] was allowed to live in the western end of the temple, where he entertained in elaborate and dissolute fashion. Shortly afterwards, Lachares robbed the cult statue of its gold.[14] Another calamity was a fire which necessitated repairs, as dowels for the statue pedestal and plaster additions to the echini of the interior colonnade show.[15] Under Nero a large inscription honoring the emperor was placed on the eastern architrave, and later Hadrian was thanked for his bounties by having his statue set up in the cella. Sometime after the edict of Theodosius II in A.D. 426 ordering the destruction of pagan temples, the statue of Athena[16] seems to have disappeared. Later an apse was made at the eastern end at the expense of the wall and frieze; side doors were cut, a gallery was built, and the Parthenon became a Greek Catholic church.

In 1209 it was changed to a Roman Catholic church and put in charge of Bérard, Bishop of Athens, a Frenchman. In 1458 the Turks turned it into a mosque, adding a minaret and making other changes. It was fortunate that travelers made drawings of it, for in 1687 the Venetians, informed by a Turkish deserter that the Turks kept their powder there, directed their guns at it and caused an explosion which played particular havoc with the sides. Then the Venetian leader, Francesco Morosini, eager to take part of the western pediment home as spoils of war, lowered some of the figures with makeshift equipment, which gave way under the strain and smashed them. Shortly after 1688, when Athens again fell into the hands of the Turks, a small mosque was built inside the remains of the temple.

---

[11] The building inscription gives the salaries of the sculptors working on the pediments, evidence against the theory that these statues were actually carved by Pheidias.
[12] See Praschniker, "Die Akroterien des Parthenon," *Oest. Jahresh.*, xiii (1910), pp. 5 ff.
[13] Plutarch *Life of Demetrios* xxiii.3.
[14] Pausanias 1.25.7.
[15] Dinsmoor, *op. cit.*, pp. 93–106.
[16] Either the original by Pheidias or a copy; see Dinsmoor, *loc. cit.*

THE PARTHENON AT ATHENS

At the close of the eighteenth century the Akropolis was in ruins and Athens almost deserted. Scattered Turkish houses grew up near the Parthenon and the Erechtheion. It was then that Lord Elgin removed most of the sculptures to England and the British Museum purchased them. Since then excavation and good and bad reconstruction have been its portion.

REFERENCES
The star * indicates the most important sources for the study of the temple

CARPENTER, R., "New Material for the West Pediment of the Parthenon," *Hesperia*, I (1932), pp. 1–30; "The Lost Statues of the East Pediment," *ibid.*, II (1933), pp. 1–88.

*COLLIGNON, M., *Le Parthénon*, Paris [1912].

DINSMOOR, W. B., *Athenian Architecture in the Age of Pericles*, in preparation.

DÖRPFELD, W., "Der ältere Parthenon," *Ath. Mitt.*, XVII (1892), pp. 158–189; "Die Zeit des ältere Parthenon," *ibid.*, XXVII (1902), pp. 379–416.

LETHABY, W. R., *Greek Buildings Represented by Fragments in the British Museum*, London, 1908.

MICHAELIS, A., *Der Parthenon*, Leipzig, 1871.

*PENROSE, F. C., *An Investigation of the Principles of Athenian Architecture*, London, 1888.

*SMITH, A. H., *The Sculptures of the Parthenon*, London, 1910.

TSCHIRA, A., "Die unfertigen Säulentrommeln auf der Akropolis zu Athen," *Jahrb.*, LV (1940), pp. 242 ff.

THE TEMPLE OF POSEIDON AT SOUNION

ABOUT 444-440 B.C. PLATES XXXV AND XXXVI

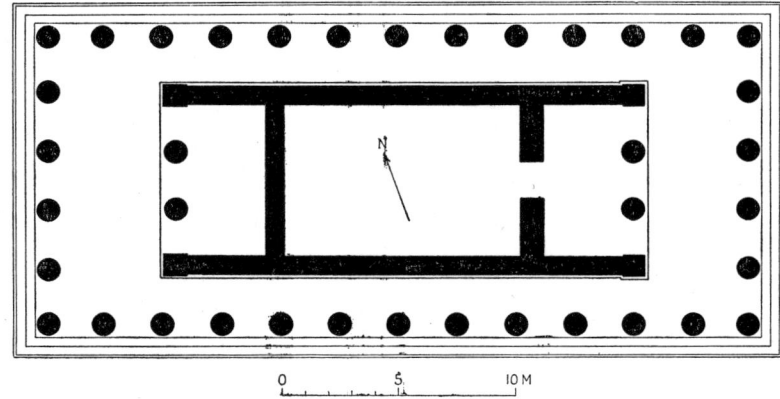

DORIC, HEXASTYLE, WITH THIRTEEN COLUMNS ON THE FLANK
STYLOBATE 44 ft. 2 in. x 102 ft. 1 in. (13.46 m. x 31.11 m.)

POSEIDON, the God of the Sea, who was worsted by Athena in the contest for a patron deity of Athens, had as one of his sanctuaries the highest spot on Cape Sounion. Here a temple to him commanded a view of ships going from Athens to the east or north (pl. xxxvi, c), and here Athenians came every four years for a nautical festival in his honor. Skippers who had trouble rounding the cape could anchor and make sacrifice to Poseidon, or in post-classical times, take away pieces of his disintegrating temple as ballast.

Two early temples are known to have existed at Sounion: a small Temple of Athena and a poros, colonnaded Temple of Poseidon. Like the pre-Parthenon, the latter was probably destroyed by the Persians before it was finished and the stone re-used in the succeeding building. Near its eastern end were found four bases and two archaic male statues.[1] These four or five or six statues (it is not certain whether the bases belong to either of the statues) antedate the poros temple; and like it they probably suffered from the Persian attack.

The present temple on the site was only slightly larger than its predecessor (pl. xxxv, A and B). It was built of marble from Agrileza, a quarry north of Sounion, just off the main highway to the famous silver mines at Laurion.[2] Unlike the Pentelic, this marble contains no iron, so that the columns today are still white and gleaming. The shafts, with only sixteen flutes and without entasis, are similar in proportion to those of the Hephaisteion in Athens (see pl. xxx, B). Like the latter, the Sounion temple had a frieze above either porch (pl. xxxv, c). The western end is destroyed, but at the east the architrave blocks in situ show that the frieze extended all the way across the pteroma to the colonnade, as in the Hephaisteion. Enough of the frieze remains to suggest that it ran all the way around the pronaos and opisthodomos, but this is

---

[1] K. A. Rhomaios, *Antike Denkmäler*, IV, pls. 47-56.
[2] See Frazer, *Pausanias*, vol. II, pp. 4-6, for the importance of these mines to Athens.

THE TEMPLE OF POSEIDON AT SOUNION

not certain. The slabs are too much broken and weathered to give an adequate idea of the arrangement, but the subjects seem to be the combat of Centaurs and Lapiths, the battle of gods and giants, and the exploits of Theseus. A Lesbian kymation decorated the top of the architrave beneath it. On the fascia crowning the back of the architrave there was a painted double guilloche.[3] Of the pediment sculptures nothing certain remains though a seated draped figure (pl. xxxvi, B) found on the site may have belonged to one of the groups. The lengths of the cella and the opisthodomos are conjectural, as there is no trace of the dividing wall.

Spon and Wheler, who investigated the temple in 1676, made a note that fourteen peripteral columns were standing, as well as a good deal of the pronaos. LeRoy in 1754 saw thirteen peripteral columns and the two antae and columns of the pronaos. Revett and Chandler, under the auspices of the Society of Dilettanti in 1765, and Dodwell in 1805 saw twelve of the peripteral columns. The south anta had disappeared. Blouet, who visited the temple in 1829, recorded the same number of columns that are standing today—nine on the south side and two on the north, as well as an anta and column of the pronaos.

The first systematic excavations at the Temple of Poseidon were made by the German Archaeological Institute under Dörpfeld from March 17 to 30, 1884. Adequate machinery for thorough excavating was lacking, but Dörpfeld discovered the foundations of the poros temple. Since 1897 the Greek Archaeological Society under Staïs has excavated at Sounion, with the further important discovery of an inscription proving that this temple was the Temple of Poseidon, not the Temple of Athena as it was formerly thought to be. In 1906 the two archaic "Apollos" mentioned above were discovered, and in 1908 the fallen anta in the pronaos was reconstructed. Whether one sees it from the water or from the land, as Byron preferred to see it, the temple is a sight of great majesty and beauty (pl. xxxvi, A).

[3] W. Zschietzschmann, "Zum innen Architrave von Sunion," *Arch. Anz.*, XLIV (1929), pp. 221–225.

REFERENCES
The star * indicates the most important sources for the study of the temple

BLOUET, A., *Expédition scientifique de Morée* (Paris, 1838), vol. III, pp. 15 ff.

DINSMOOR, W. B., "The Temple of Ares at Athens," *Hesperia*, IX (1940), pp. 1 ff.

*DÖRPFELD, W., "Der Tempel von Sounion," *Ath. Mitt.*, IX (1884), pp. 324 ff.

FABRICIUS, E., "Die Skulpturen vom Tempel in Sounion," *Ath. Mitt.*, IX (1884), pp. 338 ff.

FRAZER, *Pausanias*, vol. II, pp. 1 ff.

ORLANDOS, A., "The Pediment of the Temple of Poseidon at Sounion (in Greek)," Δελτίον, 1915, pp. 1–27.

*———, "The Walls and Roof of the Temple of Poseidon at Sounion (in Greek)," Ἀρχαιολογικὴ Ἐφημερίς (1917), pp. 213 ff.

SOCIETY OF DILETTANTI, *The Unedited Antiquities of Attica* (London, 1833), pp. 53 ff.

*STAÏS, V., "Excavations in Sounion (in Greek)," Ἀρχαιολογικὴ Ἐφημερίς (1900), pp. 113 ff; *ibid.*, 1917, pp. 168 ff.

THE TEMPLE AT EGESTA (SEGESTA)

ABOUT 420 B. C. PLATES XXXVII AND XXXVIII

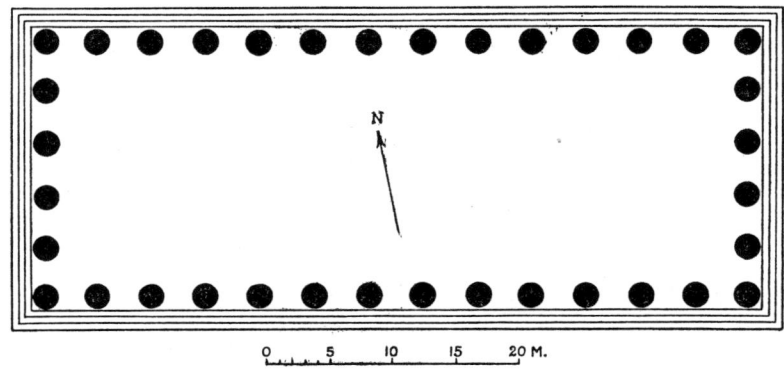

DORIC, HEXASTYLE, WITH FOURTEEN COLUMNS ON THE FLANK
STYLOBATE 75 ft. 10 in. x 190 ft. 5 in. (23.12 m. x 58.04 m.)

PERCHED on the side of a mountain in northwestern Sicily, with no modern town near by to add a discordant note, and surrounded by mountains, is one of the most beautiful of temple ruins, the temple at Segesta, called Egesta by the Greeks (pl. XXXVIII, c). It can scarcely be classed as a ruin, for its entire colonnade and both pediments are still in place. How much of it has been destroyed is problematical. If there is any truth in the theory that the colonnade was the first part of a temple to be constructed, perhaps its cella was never completed; at any rate there remains no trace of it (pl. XXXVII, B). The columns were never fluted, nor was the temple ever stuccoed. The bosses for use in lifting many of its heavy blocks were not removed (pl. XXXVIII, A and B), and the joints were not dressed.

The temple, which was planned with great refinement of line and executed with precision in local shell-conglomerate, must have been an arresting sight from the city below. The curve of the stylobate (3⅛ inches in 200 feet) may be seen in plate XXXVIII, B; several writers have stated that there is a curve in plan, or horizontal plane.[1] The abaci are tilted slightly forward, and the strong diminution of the columns suggests that entasis was intended after the fluting was finished. The second and third columns from each end depart from the normal intercolumniation by being closer to the end column, one way of solving the problem of spacing triglyphs and metopes at the corners. Not a trace of sculptured or painted ornament has been found except the palmette shown on page 41, which Hittorff and Zanth discovered underneath a corner of the cornice. No altar has been unearthed before the temple, nor is the god known to whom it was dedicated.

The city of Segesta was called Egesta in pre-Roman times. Its inhabitants were the Elymoi, people who came from Troy originally, according to tradition, and settled here and at Eryx.[2] Like the inhabitants of all the jealous cities of Sicily, Egesta had no communal feeling and did not hesitate to call in outsiders to help fight a neighbor. About 580 B.C. the Phoenicians helped her successfully against Selinus, which in turn was supported by Rhodians and Cnidians. In about 510 B.C., again with the help of Carthage, Egesta

---

[1] Dinsmoor doubts this. [2] Thucydides VI.11.3.

THE TEMPLE AT EGESTA (SEGESTA)

expelled the Spartan prince Dorieus, in spite of the fact that the Delphic oracle had said Dorieus would win.[3] In 416 Egesta appealed to Athens, on whom she had no claim, against Syracuse and Selinus, and when the Athenian expedition failed, she called in Carthage. She was thus on the winning side in 409 and 406, when Carthage defeated Selinus and Akragas. Carthage, having then a firm foothold on the island, began to devastate various cities, including Egesta.

This calamity and the subsequent annihilation of the city by the tyrant Agathokles makes the survival of so much of this temple a monument to the sound construction of Greek buildings. In Roman times the city was rebuilt, named Segesta, and became a place of some importance. The theater with its exquisite, natural backdrop was altered, as were so many Greek theaters in Roman times. Later the Saracens attacked the town but spared the temple, fortunately for the few tourists who venture into the mountains to see it.

[3] Herodotos v.43–48.

REFERENCES
The star * indicates the most important sources for the study of the temple

*Hittorff, J. I., and Zanth, L., *Recueil des monuments de Ségeste et de Sélinonte*, Paris, 1870.

*Koldewey, R., and Puchstein, O., *Die griechischen Tempel in Unteritalien und Sicilien*, Berlin, 1899.

Randall-MacIver, D., *Greek Cities in Italy and Sicily*. Oxford, 1931.

THE TEMPLE OF ATHENA NIKE AT ATHENS

BETWEEN 427–424 B. C.   PLATES XXXIX AND XL

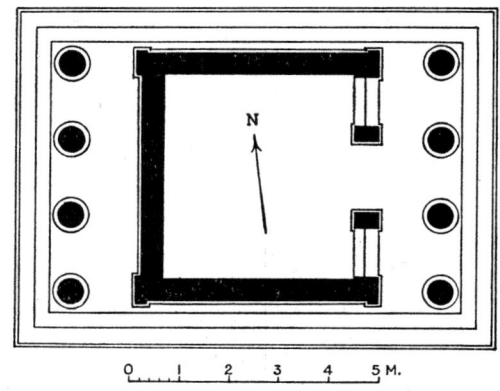

IONIC, AMPHIPROSTYLE, TETRASTYLE
STYLOBATE 17 ft. 8½ in. x 26 ft. 5½ in. (5.40 m. x 8.17 m.)

CLIMBING up to the Propylaia, the only means of entrance to the Akropolis at Athens, one sees to the right and above the Temple of Athena Nike (pl. XL, A). Although it lacks the carefully planned curves of the Parthenon, its proportions are good and its restrained decoration is most pleasing. It commands a magnificent view of the Aegean gulf; Pausanias[1] tells us that here Aigeus looked for the sail of his son, Theseus, who had journeyed to Crete to kill the Minotaur, and that here he threw himself down the steep incline when a black sail made him think that Theseus was dead.

The history of the Temple of Athena Nike (Athena in the guise of Victory) is closely bound up with that of the Propylaia. Apparently for years there had been a temple and altar of Athena Nike on this site, perhaps housing the wooden statue of Athena that Pausanias mentions.[2] A building inscription of 449 B.C. orders the building of a marble temple and altar to Athena Nike by Kallikrates, but this work was apparently held up by Perikles's decision to rebuild the entire Akropolis and does not seem to have been begun until after work on the Propylaia was terminated.

Kallikrates, then, who had to his credit his work on the Parthenon, was the architect of the Temple of Athena Nike. Mnesikles was the architect of the Propylaia and seems also to have supervised the Erechtheion, begun probably soon after the Temple of Athena Nike. Working within a stone's throw of each other, they were apparently professional as well as political rivals. Each wanted every inch of land he could possibly get. Mnesikles was hampered by the sanctuary of Artemis Brauronia on the southeast and the sanctuary of Athena Nike on the southwest in carrying out his brilliant plan for a large and symmetrical gateway to the Akropolis. Kallikrates's work was limited by the smallness of the platform on which he had to build and the nearness of the Propylaia. He very wisely built a small and simple temple with one portico

---
[1] I.22.4–5.
[2] V.26.6. Remains of an earlier temple and its retaining wall were found in 1936 during the reconstruction of the temple. The altar belonging to this poros building had been discovered previously.

THE TEMPLE OF ATHENA NIKE AT ATHENS

facing the Akropolis and the other looking toward the sea and the distant coast of the Peloponnese.

The axis of the Temple of Athena Nike was not parallel to the Propylaia or the Parthenon but had an orientation all its own. The pronaos was inclosed by a grille. The frieze, of Pentelic marble like the temple, is carved on thick blocks instead of the usual thin facings which were cheaper and more easily transported, and to this its preservation is no doubt due. On the front it shows a council of gods and perhaps heroes (pl. xxxix, A), a theme similar to that of the Hephaisteion and Parthenon friezes, while on the sides are battle scenes of Greeks fighting Greeks and Greeks fighting Persians.[3] Four blocks of this frieze are in the British Museum but have been replaced by copies. The sima had a painted palmette design between lion-head waterspouts, and there was perhaps sculpture on the pediments, as traces of dowels on the cornice indicate, but nothing remains of this. The cult statue, which was of wood, represented Athena with a pomegranate in her right hand and a helmet in her left. She was wingless, as usual, a fact which caused the temple to be miscalled for a good many years the Temple of the Wingless Victory. To the east of the temple are remains of an altar where cows selected especially for their beauty were sacrificed to the goddess.

The famous parapet of sculptured Victories (pl. xxxix, B and C), built around the dizzy platform on which the temple stands, was constructed after the temple, as cuttings on the backs of the slabs show. It was surmounted by a metal grille, holes for the insertion of which, together with dowel-, clamp-, and pry-holes, have enabled Dinsmoor to work out a scheme for the sculptured slabs and assign them to several unknown sculptors. Accordingly it appears that the lovely Nike binding her sandal (pl. xxxix, C) was placed on the south side, where, unfortunately, almost no one would have noticed her. The parapet formed an arm at the steps on the northeast and ran around the temple to the south side where it was probably continued beyond the temple to the wall of the Propylaia. About 410 B.C. seems a probable date for the parapet.

Like the Athenian Treasury at Delphi, the present Temple of Athena Nike is a reconstruction. After having served as a powder magazine, the original was destroyed by the Turks about 1686 and made into a battery, but as enough vestiges were left to show its plan, it was rebuilt in 1835 by Ross, Schaubert, and Hansen. From time to time since then other parts of it have been discovered. In 1935 the temple was dismembered by the Greek Archaeological Society and several fragments of the parapet, including a full-length figure of a Nike, were unearthed; the reconstruction was completed in 1940 (pl. xl, B).

[3] Perhaps the battle of Plataea. See the casts of this frieze in the Metropolitan Museum.

REFERENCES

The star * indicates the most important sources for the study of the temple

BLÜMEL, C., *Der Fries des Tempels der Athena Nike*, Berlin, 1923.

CARPENTER, R., *The Sculpture of the Nike Temple Parapet*, Cambridge [Mass.], 1929.

*DINSMOOR, W. B., *Athenian Architecture in the Age of Pericles*, in preparation.

*————, "The Sculptured Parapet of Athena Nike," A.J.A., xxx (1926), pp. 1 ff.

*————, "The Nike Parapet Once More," A.J.A., xxxiv (1930), pp. 281 ff.

LETHABY, W. R., *Greek Buildings Represented by Fragments in the British Museum*, London, 1908.

ORLANDOS, A., "Zum Tempel der Athena Nike," *Ath. Mitt.*, xl (1915), pp. 27 ff.

ROSS, L., SCHAUBERT, E., and HANSEN, C., *Der Tempel der Nike Apteros*, Berlin, 1839.

SHOE, *Profiles*, pl. lxxviii.

SMITH, A. H., *Catalogue of Sculpture in the Department of Greek and Roman Antiquities, British Museum*, vol. 1 (1892), pp. 239 ff.

*STEVENS, G. P., "The Cornice of the Temple of Athena Nike," A.J.A., xii (1908), pp. 398 ff.

WELTER, G., "Vom Nikepyrgos," *Ath. Mitt.*, xlviii (1923), pp. 190 ff.

THE ARGIVE HERAION

ABOUT 423–410 B. C.   PLATES XLI AND XLII

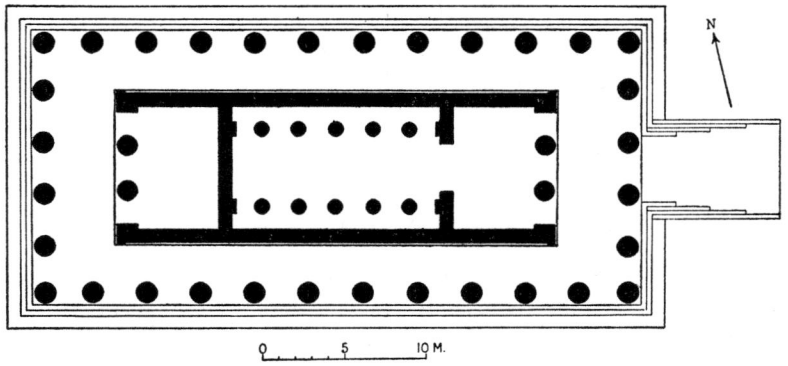

DORIC, HEXASTYLE, WITH TWELVE COLUMNS ON THE FLANK
STYLOBATE 57 ft. 2 in. x 121 ft. 5 in. (17.42 m. x 37.01 m.)

ABOUT three miles from Mycenae and five from Argos was the famous sanctuary of Hera, belonging, according to Strabo,[1] to both these cities. At this sanctuary Agamemnon is said to have been chosen leader of the Greeks in the Trojan War,[2] and here from early times games were held, ending in a procession in honor of Hera. The cult statue by Polykleitos in the Heraion was "in execution the most beautiful in the world" though in costliness and size inferior to the famous cult statues by Pheidias.[1]

Remains of two temples of Hera have been found, the earlier one dating from the beginning of the seventh century B.C. Even though we have no evidence of preceding temples which probably existed on the spot, we have records of two priestesses. One was Kydippe, the mother of those dutiful youths, Kleobis and Biton, who, when oxen could not be brought quickly enough to take her to her duties at the temple, drew the cart themselves. The other was Chryseis, who accidentally caused the temple to be destroyed by fire when she fell asleep and a lamp ignited some wreaths. She then fled to Tegea and took refuge in the sanctuary of Athena Alea. Only the platform with markings where the wooden columns stood and bits of charred wood remain of the temple, but it was probably of much the same construction as the Heraion at Olympia.

The new Temple of Hera must have been started in 423 B.C., immediately after the fire. The people of Argos and near-by places reckoned time by the years of office of the priestesses of Hera, so it would not have done to let Hera be without a temple there. The terrace below the old temple was leveled, and here the new temple was constructed, probably replacing an old altar. Eupolemos of Argos was the architect.

The temple was built of stuccoed limestone with carved decoration and roof tiles of marble. A ramp led up to the eastern door, and the porches were distyle in antis. The echinus profile resembles that of the Parthenon, and the akroteria seem to have been made up of a rinceau design similar to those of the Parthenon but there may have been figures also, as at Aigina. The sima was carved, instead of being painted as was usual, in a design of palmettes and scrolls on which perched cuckoos (pl. XLII, A). The cuckoo was sacred to

[1] VIII.6.10.   [2] *Dictys Cretensis* I.16.

THE ARGIVE HERAION

Hera, for it was in the form of this bird that Zeus first appeared to her.[3] Many lion-head waterspouts have been found, more or less fragmentary.

The remains of the sculpture of the pediments and metopes are numerous but so broken that the decorative scheme can only be conjectured (pl. XLII, c). According to Pausanias the Birth of Zeus decorated the eastern pediment (pl. XLI, A), and the Capture of Troy the western one. Sculptured metopes apparently adorned all four sides of the temple, the subjects being the battle of the gods and giants and the contest of Greeks and Amazons. The base of the cult statue has been discovered, but the coins of Argos (pl. XLII, B) and the description by Pausanias are all we have to give us an idea of this famous chryselephantine statue. The goddess was seated, holding in one hand a scepter and in the other a pomegranate (pl. XLI, B); on her head was a crown with the Graces and Seasons wrought on it in relief; and near her stood a statue of Hebe by Naukydes. Both Hera and Hebe are shown on Roman coins of Argos.

The Heraion commanded a wide view of the Argive plain (pl. XLII, D), and with the buildings which stood near it must have been an imposing sight. Earthquakes and despoilers reduced the sanctuary to denuded foundations, which were all that rewarded the excavators.

The site was discovered by General Gordon while on a hunting trip and excavated by him in 1836. Rangabé and Bursian, poorly supplied with funds, worked there in 1854. From 1892 to 1895 the Archaeological Institute of America and the American School of Classical Studies at Athens made a more exhaustive study, the results of which they published in 1902 and 1905.

[3] Pausanias II.17.4.

REFERENCES
The star * indicates the most important source for the study of the temple

EICHLER, F., "Die Skulpturen des Heraions bei Argos," *Oest. Jahresh.* XIX–XX (1916–1919), pp. 15–153.

FRAZER, *Pausanias*, vol. III, pp. 165 ff.

FRICKENHAUS, A., and MÜLLER, W., "Aus der Argolis," *Ath. Mitt.*, XXXVI (1911), pp. 26 ff.

*WALDSTEIN, C., and others, *The Argive Heraeum*, Boston and New York, 1902.

THE ERECHTHEION AT ATHENS

ABOUT 421–406 B. C.   PLATES XLIII AND XLIV

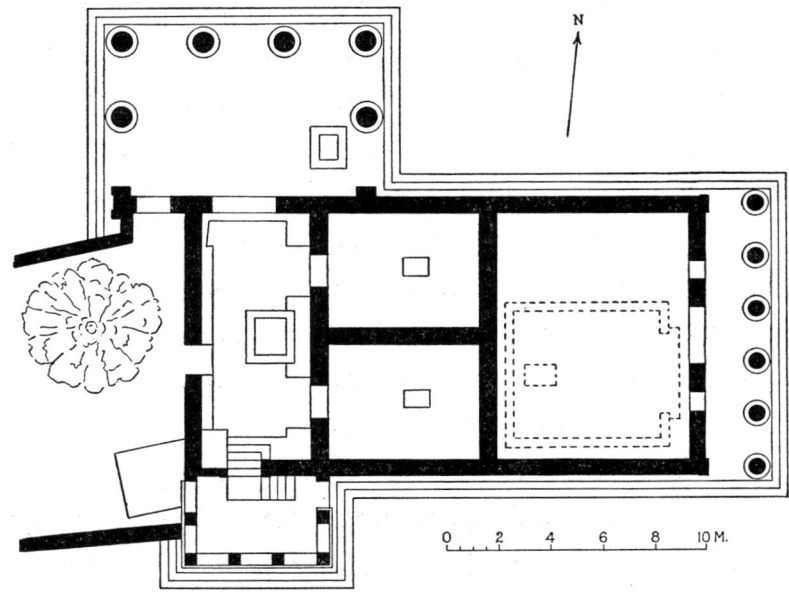

IONIC, IRREGULAR
Width of east porch on STYLOBATE 38 ft. 2 in. (11.63 m.), maximum length from east to west on STYLOBATE 83 ft. 10 in. (25.56 m.)

NORTH of the Old Temple of Athena and not on an axis with it stands the Erechtheion, perhaps the successor to the former after its partial destruction by the Persians in 479 B.C. Mnesikles was probably the architect of this graceful Ionic building, whose plan, as well as Pausanias's method in describing it, have been the subject of much discussion. Dörpfeld believed that it was designed twice as large originally but curtailed because of the opposition of the conservatives and the priests to the destruction of the sacred tokens at the western end of its site. A logical theory is that it succeeded the Old Temple of Athena as the shrine of Athena and Erechtheus, after the ancient image of Athena Polias was returned from its place of refuge in Salamis at the end of the Persian War.[1] A temporary canopy was perhaps erected for the cult statue northeast of the Old Temple of Athena, and around this was built the eastern cella of the Erechtheion with its beautiful porch.

Behind this cella, on a lower level, were three rooms, closely paralleling the arrangement in the Old Temple of Athena; of the two inner rooms one contained an altar of Boutes, the other an altar of Hephaistos. Judging by the probable arrangement of marble doors and a grille above the low wall separating these rooms from the west room, Mnesikles may have planned them to hold the treasure, but they never replaced the near-by Opisthodomos as a treasury.

In the third, or western, room, which was entered by the north and Caryatid porches, the difficulties and ingenuity of the architect are abundantly evident. The sacred tokens which he had to avoid were: 1) The marks of Poseidon's trident when he struck the rock. These may have been on the spot over which

[1] Dinsmoor, A.J.A., XXXVI (1932), pp. 318 ff.

the architect built the north portico with open spaces in the roof, ceiling, and floor (see plan and pl. XLIII, A) so that the sacred relic might be left uncovered. A door, with a lintel reinforced by iron to carry the weight of the north wall of the temple led to the crypt so formed.[2] This sacred structure has also been thought to be the altar of Zeus Hypatos or of the Thyechous. 2) The sanctuary of Pandrosos, daughter of Kekrops, the traditional founder of Athens. This was left to the west of the Erechtheion. The north portico and northwest corner of the building were constructed on its retaining wall, and a small door from the north portico led to it. 3) The olive tree which Athena created in her contest with Poseidon. This remained outside the building, somewhere near the Pandroseion. 4) The salt sea which sprang up when Poseidon struck the rock. The stairs leading down to it were protected from the rain by the Caryatid porch, or Porch of the Maidens, and the western room was built over it. 5) The legendary grave or sanctuary of Kekrops, which caused great complications. This apparently curtailed the length of the building, changed the proposed size of the western room, threw the north and south doors off axis, and weakened the south end of the west wall by necessitating a long spanning lintel. It must have hidden part of the west wall, for that is unfinished (pl. XLIII, B), and part of the podium of the Caryatid porch, as the moldings were never carved.

Around the entire building and porches—except the Porch of the Maidens—were delicately carved moldings and a frieze (pls. XLIII and XLIV, A).[3] The frieze was unusual in having white marble figures doweled onto a black limestone backing. The section over the north porch was slightly taller than that of the rest of the building. The remains of the sculpture are so fragmentary that the subjects are hard to distinguish, but an assembly of deities probably decorated the east end, as in the Hephaisteion, the Parthenon, and the Temple of Athena Nike. The presence of horses, mentioned in the building inscriptions, seems probable, as the horse was a creation of Poseidon; moreover Erechtheus was the first to harness a horse and is said to have introduced horse racing in the Panathenaic games.

The porches of the Erechtheion are famous for the beauty of their details, which have been adapted for countless later buildings. A column from the east portico with its beautifully carved capital is in the British Museum, as is one of the Caryatids, whose place is taken by a copy in Portland cement. The Porch of the Maidens (pl. XLIV, B) was apparently not a much used one, as its step is carved in a molding which would be more worn had it been a public entrance. That this portico is so small is an argument for the theory that the Old Temple of Athena remained in use as the Opisthodomos after the Persians destroyed the eastern end. The columns of the north porch (pl. XLIII, C) have a very subtle entasis called by Penrose "the most delicate line which had probably ever been applied in architecture." The guilloches of the capitals had inserts of glass, and bronze hooks for garlands were fastened to the volutes. Its much copied doorway was repaired in Roman and Byzantine times.

Funds were scarce at the time of the building of the Erechtheion on account of the Peloponnesian War, and so practically every penny spent on the temple was accounted for in the building inscriptions.[4] These are accordingly valuable records of Greek architectural methods. It was these that enabled Dörpfeld to estimate the length of the Attic foot (between 0.326 and 0.328 m.) by comparison with other buildings. They make no mention of when the temple was begun, but they do show that in 409 B.C. a survey of the

---

[2] Dinsmoor, *A.J.A.*, XXVI (1922), p. 151.
[3] The Metropolitan Museum of Art owns two fragments of egg-and-dart carving from this temple.
[4] See Stevens and others, *The Erechtheum*, pp. 277 ff. Supervising architects, sculptors, etc., received one drachma a day in Athens at this time; see Richter, *Sculpture*, p. 160.

unfinished work and the materials on hand was taken. Apparently there had been a delay in the building, perhaps from 415 to 409 on account of the ruinous Sicilian expedition. The subsequent records are fragmentary lists of expenses, but evidently the building was completed, except for a few details, about 406 B.C.

Like the Parthenon the Erechtheion suffered many misfortunes in the course of time, including at least two fires—in 376 B.C.[5] and in the Augustan period—after which it was repaired. Since the Roman period it has been successively used as a Christian church, a Turkish dwelling, and a powder magazine, which barely missed being set on fire when the explosion occurred in the Parthenon. It also served as a quarry for lead, iron, and stone for secular buildings. Extensive study of the temple was made from 1905 to 1920 by the American School at Athens, and during the same time restorations were made by the Greek government.

[5] Dinsmoor, A.J.A., xxxvi (1932), pp. 325 ff.

REFERENCES

The star * indicates the most important sources for the study of the temple

*DINSMOOR, W. B., "The Burning of the Opisthodomos," A.J.A., xxxvi (1932), pp. 143 ff., 307 ff.

*DÖRPFELD, W., "Zum Erechtheion," Ath. Mitt., xxviii (1903), pp. 465 ff.; "Der ursprüngliche Plan des Erechtheion," ibid., xxix (1904), pp. 101 ff.; "Zu den Bauwerken Athens, Erechtheion und alter Tempel," ibid., xxxvi (1911), pp. 39-49; "Das Hekatompedon in Athen," Jahrb., xxxiv (1919), pp. 1 ff.; "Zum ursprünglichen Plan des Erechtheion, eine Entgegnung," Neue Jahrbücher für das klassische Altertum, Geschichte, und deutsche Litteratur und für Pädagogik, XLVII (1921), pp. 433 ff.; Book Review in Philologische Wochenschrift, XLVIII (1928), pp. 1062 ff.; cf. also Ath. Mitt., xxii (1897), p. 166, and xxvii (1902), pp. 401, 414.

ELDERKIN, G. W., Book Review in A.J.A., xxxi (1927), pp. 522 ff.

———, "The Cults of the Erechtheion," Hesperia, x (1941), pp. 113 ff.

HOLLAND, L. B., "Erechtheum Papers," A.J.A., xxviii (1924), pp. 1-23, 142-169, 402-434.

RODENWALDT, G., "Die Form des Erechtheions," Neue Jahrbücher für das klassische Altertum, Geschichte, und deutsche Litteratur und für Pädagogik, XLVII (1921), pp. 1-13.

*STEVENS, G. P., and others, The Erechtheum, Cambridge [Mass.], 1927.

WELLER, C. H., "The Original Plan of the Erechtheum," A.J.A., xxv (1921), pp. 130 ff.

THE TEMPLE OF ASKLEPIOS AT EPIDAUROS

ABOUT 380 B. C.   PLATES XLV AND XLVI

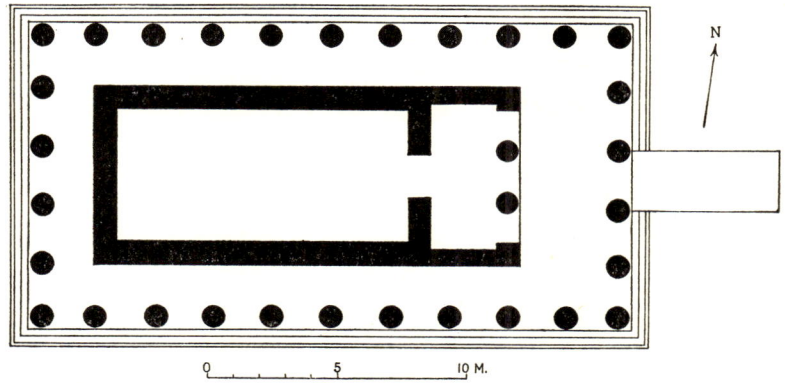

DORIC, HEXASTYLE, WITH ELEVEN COLUMNS ON THE FLANK
STYLOBATE 39 ft. 8 in. x 75 ft. 11 in. (12.09 m. x 23.14 m.)

WE are told by Pausanias[1] that Asklepios, god of healing, was born at Epidauros and that his most famous sanctuaries were offshoots of the temple there. The numerous remains at Epidauros give a hint of the scale of the sanctuary; the architectural details in the local museum and the well-preserved theater give an idea of its beauty. Here medicine was practiced by means of strange miracles performed by Asklepios, accounts of which, written on stelae, have come down to us as the earliest form of clinical records.[2]

From the descriptions of Epidauros by ancient writers we get the impression of an ancient counterpart to the modern town of Lourdes. Except in winter the sanctuary was usually swarming with worshipers and pilgrims, who came to be cured or to effect a cure for someone too ill to come. After bathing in the sacred stream and sacrificing at one of the altars, they prayed devoutly before and inside the Temple of Asklepios (pl. XLV, B). When night came they went to sleep in a dormitory near by (pl. XLV, A) and were visited in a dream by the god or one of his assistants, perhaps a snake or a dog. Fabulous cures were effected, and when in the course of time people ceased giving much credence to miracles, the priests were still useful because of the medical knowledge they had acquired.

Theodotos[3] was the architect of the fourth-century temple to Asklepios, which was built on the site of an earlier one. The material was limestone, stuccoed and gaily painted. A ramp led up to the temple, which was shorter in plan than most, having no opisthodomos. The pronaos was grilled in for use as a treasury. Its door, the door and ceiling of the cella, and the cult statue were all by Thrasymedes of Paros. The outside door was inlaid with many kinds of wood; the inner door was of various woods with ivory

---

[1] II.26.8.
[2] Frazer, *Pausanias*, vol. III, p. 248 ff., and Cavvadias, *Fouilles d'Épidaure*, pp. 23 ff. For private case records, cf. Hippokrates *Epidemics* I.III.
[3] According to the building inscriptions, this architect received about a drachma a day for four and a half years, and at the end of that time, as the pediment sculptures were not in place, he stayed on to finish the work. See Cavvadias, *op. cit.*, pp. 17, 84.

inlay and gold and gilt-bronze trimmings. Marble lion heads served as waterspouts and the marble horizontal sima was decorated with a carved rinceau design. The sculptured pediments and akroteria were of Pentelic marble and were executed by four sculptors, of whom Timotheos, who also worked on the Mausoleum at Halikarnassos, was one.[4] This artist executed a set of akroteria and some unidentified reliefs; perhaps the Nike (pl. XLVI, B) on the apex of the western pediment and two Nereids on horseback on the corners of the same pediment are by him, as well as two reliefs of Asklepios (pl. XLVI, A).[5] The other sculptural remains, except for an Amazon from the western pediment, are fragmentary. The subject of this pediment was the battle of the Greeks and Amazons; the eastern one represented the combat of the Lapiths and Centaurs. The metopes were unadorned, except perhaps for painting.

The chryselephantine cult statue was half the size of the statue of Zeus Olympios at Athens. We can get an idea of the pose of the god from coins of Epidauros reproducing the statue and from the two reliefs mentioned above. Asklepios was seated on a throne near which lay his dog; his left hand held his staff and his right rested on the head of a serpent.

Asklepios was a benevolent god who punished those who scoffed at his miracles but was surprisingly quick to forgive. He was gentle and unharassed by the many demands on him. His skill at surgery made post-operative treatment unnecessary, and his versatility was limitless. He cured the blind, the lame, the childless. Nor was he above less serious operations, such as removing from a man's stomach several leeches which his mother-in-law had put in his wine. Each grateful patient who could afford it had a slab recording his cure set up in the sanctuary. Any failure to give the god his promised reward was usually punished by a return of the malady.

In Roman times the sanctuary flourished. Just before Pausanias's visit in the second century A.D. several much needed buildings were added, including some outside the sanctuary to take care of births and deaths. The sanctuary itself was never allowed to be polluted by such events. After the fourth century A.D., when Theodosius I ordered the destruction of pagan temples, small Byzantine churches sprang up and Christian saints of healing were worshiped there. The Temple of Asklepios was finally leveled by an earthquake and then gradually dismembered by peasants seeking building material, by pirates, and by souvenir-hunters.

Epidauros was visited by Desmonceaux in 1669 and by other travelers in the eighteenth and early nineteenth centuries who, with the help of Pausanias, recognized the remains. In 1881 the Greek Archaeological Society under Cavvadias began excavating. They uncovered first the theater (pl. XLVI, C), which is the best-preserved building, next the tholos, and in 1883 the Temple of Asklepios.

[4] See Richter, *Sculpture*, pp. 274 ff., for arguments against the theory that Timotheos was the chief sculptor of the temple.
[5] See the casts in The Metropolitan Museum of Art.

REFERENCES

The star * indicates the most important sources for the study of the temple

*CAVVADIAS, P., *Fouilles d'Épidaure*, Athens, 1891.
———, *The Shrine of Asklepios in Epidaurus* (in Greek), Athens, 1900.
———, "On the Temple of Asklepios (in Greek)," Πρακτικά, (1905), pp. 43 ff.
———, "On the Excavations and Work at Epidauros (in Greek)," Πρακτικά, (1906), pp. 91 ff.
*DEFRASSE, A., and LECHAT, H., *Épidaure*, Paris, 1895.

THE TEMPLE OF ATHENA ALEA AT TEGEA

ABOUT 360–350 B.C.   PLATES XLVII AND XLVIII

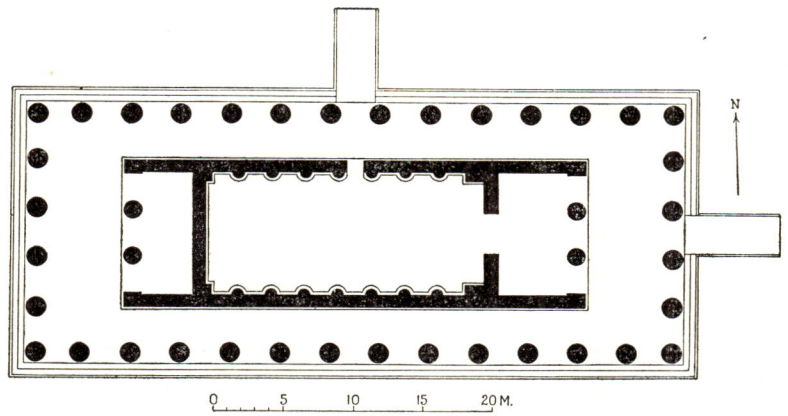

DORIC, HEXASTYLE, WITH FOURTEEN COLUMNS ON THE FLANK
STYLOBATE 62 ft. 10 in. x 155 ft. 11 in. (19.15 m. x 47.52 m.)

ONLY a few scattered stones mark the site of the Temple of Athena Alea at Tegea, called by Pausanias the most beautiful temple in the Peloponnese (pl. XLVII, A).[1] It was the second largest temple in the Peloponnese and had certain peculiarities, some of which occur in other Arcadian temples: an extra ramp led to a small door on one of its long sides, as at Bassai and Lykosoura, and there were engaged columns in the cella as at Lousoi and Bassai (pl. XLVII, B). It combined the archaic tendency of being unusually long for its width with the late characteristics of tall slender columns (over six lower diameters high) and an almost curveless echinus profile.

Skopas was chosen as architect of this fourth-century temple, which was built to replace an earlier building burned in 395 B.C. How much of the actual carving he did himself is, of course, conjectural. He probably designed the base molding and Corinthian capitals of the cella, the sima, and other ornaments, as well as the pediment and metope sculptures (pls. XLVII, C and XLVIII, B, D, C, and A). The decoration is beautiful and varied; the Corinthian capitals are more fully developed than those of the Bassai temple and the tholos at Epidauros, but are still delightfully simple.

The very fragmentary state of the temple and its sculpture makes our picture of it incomplete. Only the foundations and a few blocks of the euthynteria are in place now (pl. XLVIII, E), but enough exists to give a key to the reconstruction of most of it. The materials were conglomerate and local Doliana marble. The external metopes were uncarved and were cut in one piece with the triglyphs out of wide blocks hollowed out to lessen the weight. Remains of the metopes of the pronaos and opisthodomos show traces of sculptural decoration, which was not carved in relief but applied somewhat in the way the Erechtheion frieze was put together. Sculptural fragments of the right size have been found but cannot be identified.

---

[1] VIII.41.8 and 45.5.

THE TEMPLE OF ATHENA ALEA AT TEGEA

The subjects, to judge from the inscriptions on the architrave, seem to have been Telephos on the west and the Kapheidai on the east.

Telephos was also the subject of the decoration of the western pediment. Here his combat with Achilles was represented, and fragments of Herakles, Atalante, and warriors have been found.[2] The largest piece of sculpture remaining is the figure of Atalante from the Kalydonian boar hunt on the eastern pediment, which, together with the heads found (pl. XLVIII, A), gives an idea of the individuality of Skopas's style and may actually be his work. The akroteria were probably rinceaux and palmettes on the apex and griffins at the corners.

The cult of Athena Alea seems to have been a combination of a local protective goddess, Alea, and of Athena, whose worship was probably brought down by people from the Argolid. The venerable cult statue of the goddess by Endoios, who worked in the late sixth century B.C., was carted off to Rome by Augustus. In the time of Pausanias[3] a statue of Athena between figures of Asklepios and Hygieia by Skopas stood in its place. The foundations of a large statue base are still visible.

In the fourth century A.D., Tegea was demolished by Alaric the Goth, and the ruins, lying on a low plain exposed to the floods which poured down from the mountains, were gradually buried under the alluvial soil. The Temple of Athena Alea was excavated by the Germans in 1879 and 1882, by the French in 1888 and 1889 and from 1900 to 1902, by the Greeks in 1909, and by the French again from 1910 to 1913 under Dugas, who published a description of the temple in 1924.

---

[2] See the casts in The Metropolitan Museum of Art.   [3] VIII.47.1.

REFERENCES
The star * indicates the most important source for the study of the temple

*DUGAS, C., and others, *Le Santuaire d'Aléa Athéna à Tégée au IVᵉ siècle*, Paris, 1924.

FRAZER, *Pausanias*, vol. IV, pp. 425 ff.

THE TEMPLE OF ARTEMIS AT SARDIS

SECOND HALF OF THE IV CENTURY B.C.   PLATES XLIX AND L

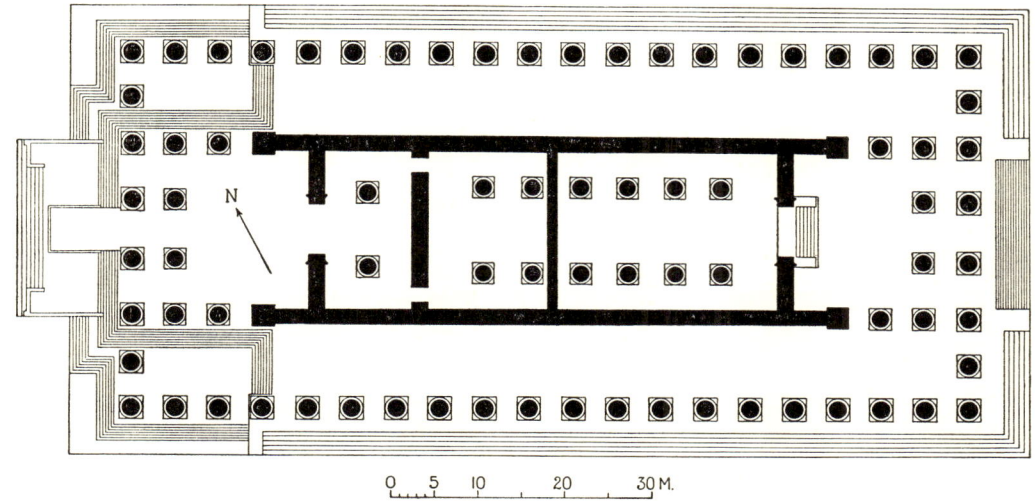

IONIC, OCTOSTYLE, WITH TWENTY COLUMNS ON THE FLANK
STYLOBATE 155 ft. 10 in. x 331 ft. 8 in. (47.50 m. x 101.09 m.)

In the Sardis room in The Metropolitan Museum of Art there are two important parts of the Temple of Artemis at Sardis, gifts of the American Society for the Excavation of Sardis. One is a column set up with most of the shaft omitted so that the exquisitely carved capital can be easily seen; the other is a reconstruction of a bit of the roof, a typical arrangement of pan-tiles and neatly fitting cover tiles. Greek temple roofs are nonexistent today and can be seen only in such reconstructions of scattered tiles or in drawings. Many roofs were burned by the Persians; some, especially the terracotta ones, disintegrated; still others were replaced by vaults when the temples became Christian churches. Pausanias tells of more than fifty temples which were either roofless or more completely ruined even in his time, the second century A.D.

The fourth-century Temple of Artemis at Sardis was built upon the foundations of an earlier temple[1] dating perhaps from the middle of the sixth century B.C., the time of Kroisos, wealthy king of Lydia. Unlike the sixth-century temple of Artemis at Ephesos, the archaic Sardis temple has left us no sculpture except an antefix to show the form of its decoration; its destruction was so thorough that we cannot tell how elaborate the decoration was which Kroisos lavished upon it. We know that this king made extravagant gifts at other shrines, that he burned couches and cups of gold to win the favor of Apollo, and that he consulted several oracles to find out whether to declare war on the Persians or not. This early temple was probably destroyed in 499 B.C. during the Ionian revolt.

The fourth-century temple of Artemis at Sardis has many points in common with the much more ambitious temple of Artemis at Ephesos. Both were octostyle, both colossal, both were apparently planned

---

[1] See Weickert, *Typen*, pp. 161 f.

with sculptured pedestals in the porches, but the Sardis ones were never carved. The Ephesos temple was dipteral, whereas the less elaborate Sardis one was pseudodipteral, at least on the sides. The peripteral shafts and capitals were larger than the elevated columns of the deep porches (pl. XLIX, A), and the bases are Asiatic Ionic with three torus designs—guilloche, upright leaves, and horizontal leaves. The capitals in the porches are unique, except for the blocks from a sixth-century temple in Chios,[2] in having palmettes carved on the eggs of one side of the echinus. A few architrave blocks have been found, as well as a lion-head waterspout and a large angle antefix. There was probably no frieze.

The cella had two rows of six columns each, now indicated solely by the plinths which supported them. Facing the east doorway as usual stood the cult statue, of which the limestone base remains. Behind this was a light cross wall which was probably removed about A.D. 141, when a colossal statue of Faustina was placed back to back with the cult statue, facing west. The treasury, west of the cella, contained two columns and may or may not have communicated with the cella.

The history of this temple is largely conjectural. The smaller size of the four elevated columns, as well as the quality of their carving, gave rise to a theory that the people of Sardis rebuilt the temple in the fifth century after its destruction in 499 B.C. It is more probable, however, that these columns were designed for the fourth-century temple and made smaller so that they could stand on sculptured bases. Most of the capitals and fluted drums (pls. XLIX, E and L, B) probably date from the fourth-century temple, while the fragments of the beautiful doorway (pl. XLIX, D),[3] the unfluted columns, and one of the two columns in situ are Roman repairs after an earthquake in the time of Tiberius (pl. L, A and B). The temple seems then to have stood intact, although unfinished in detail, until the sixth century A.D. Marble chips found in excavating show that despoiling had begun at this period. Continued looting and earth sliding down from the akropolis destroyed the temple, so that early travelers in Asia Minor noticed first six, then five, then three columns rising out of the fields near the river Paktolos. Only two were left standing when the American Society for the Excavation of Sardis dug there from 1910 to 1914.

[2] See Shoe, *Profiles*, Plates, pl. A. [3] See Shoe, *Profiles*, Text, pp. 50, 84.

REFERENCES
The star * indicates the most important source for the study of the temple

*BUTLER, H. C., *Sardis*, vol. II, part I, Leyden, 1925.
RICHTER, G. M. A., *Handbook of the Classical Collection (The Metropolitan Museum of Art)* (New York, 1930), pp. 321 ff.

VALLOIS, R., "Comptes rendus bibliographiques," *Revue des études grecques*, XXXIX (1926), pp. 367 ff.

THE TEMPLE OF APOLLO AT DIDYMA

ABOUT 334 B.C.—A.D. 41   PLATES LI AND LII

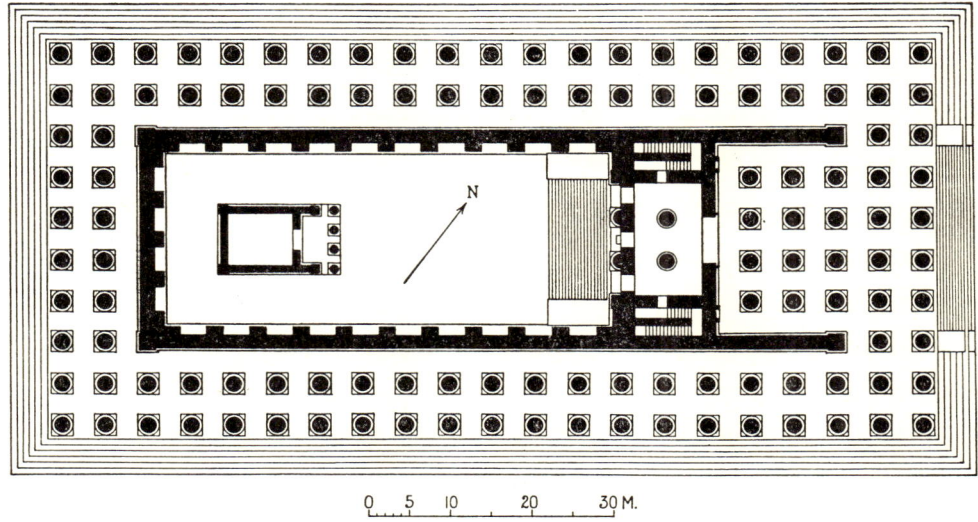

IONIC, DECASTYLE, DIPTERAL, WITH TWENTY-ONE COLUMNS ON THE FLANK
STYLOBATE 167 ft. 9 in. x 358 ft. 11 in. (51.10 m. x 109.40 m.)

WE come now to the known exception to the statement that Greek temples were probably not hypaethral. The Temple of Apollo at Didyma was, as Strabo says,[1] too large to have a roof; moreover it possessed two features that seem necessary to a hypaethral temple: its cult statue was protected from the elements by a tiny separate shrine within the temple (pl. LI, A), and a conduit for rain water has been discovered in its cella. This colossal temple also housed an oracle which had been temporarily silenced when the Persians burned its predecessor in 494 B.C.[2] Among the few relics of the archaic shrine are the seated Branchidai figures in the British Museum which flanked the approach to the temple and the fine egg-and-dart molding which crowned the retaining wall of the running track surrounding the temple.

Paionios of Ephesos, who had proved his skill in ambitious buildings in the Temple of Artemis at Ephesos, and Daphnis of Miletos were the architects of the fourth-century Temple of Apollo at Didyma. It was dipteral, with three rows of four columns each in the pronaos and no opisthodomos. The carving of the façade columns was elaborate: the bases were decorated with palmette, guilloche, and fret designs and two were dodecagonal (pl. LI, C–E), while the capitals had heads of gods in the volutes and bulls in the centers (pl. LI, B), and the two end columns in addition had griffins instead of volutes at the outer corners.[2] The tiered architrave was surmounted by an elaborate frieze with Medusa heads and rinceaux, and the dentils of the cornice were decorated with palmettes, each different from the next (pl. LI, B).

Seven steps led up to the main façade, except in the center between two pylons, where they were increased to thirteen for easy access to the temple (pl. LI, F). The huge central opening from the pronaos to

---

[1] XIV.1.5.   [2] Wiegand, *Achter vorläufiger Bericht*... p. 21, fig. 11.

the antechamber was framed with enormous blocks, and the threshold was so high (6 feet) that it could not have been meant for a doorway. The entry to the cella, fourteen feet below, was not through this opening but through much smaller doors on either side of it which opened into sloping vaulted passages.[3] The stairways shown in the plan, entered from the antechamber, were above these passages and led to upper chambers or to the roof. Whatever purpose the antechamber was used for, it was accessible only from the cella, from which a monumental stairway led up to it. Two Corinthian columns supported the ceiling of the antechamber.

The large hypaethral cella was surrounded, except on the east, by a dado and pilastered walls (pls. LI, A and LII, B). In it were a sacred spring, a house for the oracle, and a shrine, or naiskos, for Apollo. The latter was really a separate Ionic temple, tetrastyle, prostyle, and measuring about 8.59 by 14.54 meters. It housed the bronze Apollo by Kanachos, which had been carried off by Xerxes and restored by Seleukos from Ecbatana in about 295 B.C.

Records say that Alexander the Great was the person for whom the oracle of the new temple gave its first edict, an event which occurred in 331 B.C., when the temple was far from complete. From building inscriptions we know that the work dragged on and on, and the ornament points to various periods of execution, including the Pergamene and the Hadrianic. Some of the fluting, some carving of the bases, and the sima and pediment were probably never executed.

In the course of time, ravages by the Goths, fires, rebuilding on the site, and a severe earthquake about 1493 made chaos of the Temple of Apollo. Three successive Byzantine churches occupied the cella; a cistern was built in one of the inner stairways, and a graveyard nestled against the exterior stairs. Walls and defenses were erected on the ruins of the main entrance and a windmill crowned the wreck; so it is indeed amazing that three of the inner row of pteron columns are still in situ, two of them with the architrave in place. Of the many travelers who described the site Cyriacus of Ancona, an Italian, was the only one to see the temple before the earthquake of 1493.[4] In 1873 the first excavating began; Rayet and Thomas sank shafts and made measurements at the expense of the Barons de Rothschild and were able to secure several examples of the sculptured decoration for the Louvre. In 1895 and 1896 Pontremoli and Haussoullier concentrated on the main façade, bringing to light more decorative and structural details, and in 1906 the Berlin Staatliche Museen began unearthing the temple and finished the work in 1909.

[3] One of the early uses of the vault which became so popular in Roman times.
[4] Pontremoli, E., and Haussoullier. B., *Didymes*, pp. 9 f.

REFERENCES

The star * indicates the most important source for the study of the temple

*Pontremoli, E., and Haussoullier, B., *Didymes*, Paris, 1904.
Rayet, O., and Thomas, A., *Milet et la Golfe Latmique*, Paris, 1877–1880.

Wiegand, T., *Siebenter* and *Achter vorläufiger Bericht über die . . . in Milet und Didyma unternommenen Ausgrabungen* (Akademie der Wissenchaften), Berlin, 1911 and 1924.

TEMPLE OF ZEUS OLYMPIOS AT ATHENS

174 B.C.–A.D. 131   PLATES LIII AND LIV

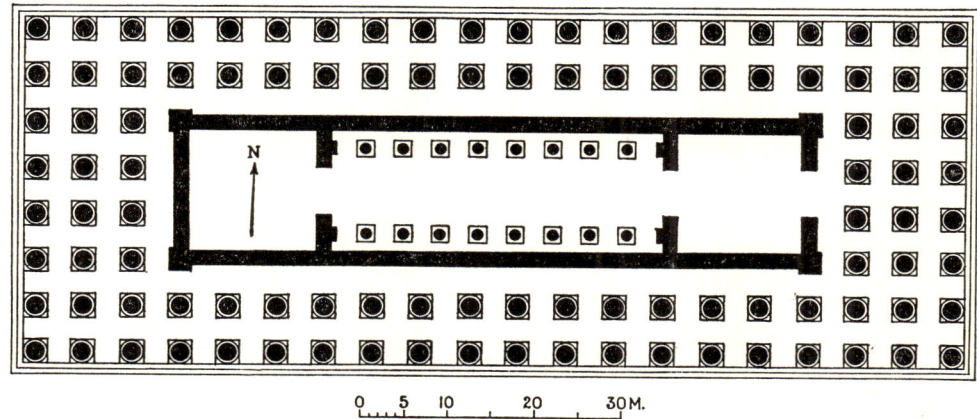

CORINTHIAN, OCTOSTYLE, WITH TWENTY COLUMNS ON THE FLANK; DIPTERAL ON THE SIDES, TRIPTERAL AT THE ENDS

STYLOBATE measuring 135 ft. 1 in. x 354 ft. 1 in. (41.17 m. x 107.92 m.)

Zeus, the Father of the Gods, had his main sanctuary at Olympia, but enough remains of two of the largest of Greek temples, the Temples of Zeus Olympios at Akragas and Athens (pl. LIV, A and B), to show what ambitious buildings were planned in his honor in other cities. It took six centuries to complete his temple at Athens; in fact, Lucian tells us that Zeus inquired whether the Athenians had any intention of ever finishing it for him.[1] "Its cult statue," Pausanias says, "surpassed in size all other images of its time except the colossi at Rhodes and at Rome."[2]

The majestic ruin in the city, southeast of the Akropolis, represents the third building on the site. The first, a much smaller temple whose foundations have been found in part, is said to have been built by Deukalion, the Greek Noah. According to Pausanias,[3] the flood in Deukalion's time ran safely away down a cleft in the ground "a cubit's width," which appeared near this spot, and a temple was thereupon erected to commemorate this event.

The second project on the spot was a huge dipteral, octostyle temple, probably Doric. It was started about 515 B.C. by the sons of Peisistratos. The architects, Vitruvius tells us,[4] were Antistates, Kallaischros, Antimachides, and Porinos. Its foundations and some unchanneled drums have been found, but no bases or capitals have come to light; apparently its construction was abandoned after the fall of the Peisistratids, as their successors were concentrating on temples to Athena on the Akropolis. Blocks prepared for it were used in other buildings and for the subsequent Corinthian temple.

In about 174 B.C. Antiochos Epiphanes undertook to rebuild this huge edifice at his own expense as a Corinthian temple (pl. LIII, A), employing Cossutius, a Roman citizen, as architect. The temple was

---

[1] *Ikaromenippos* 24.   [2] I.18.6.   [3] I.18.7.   [4] VII. Pref.15.

built of Pentelic marble from the stylobate up. The substructure of the outer peribolos of the previous temple was a hollow rectangle, but each inside column had its separate foundation. When the new equally spaced columns did not fall on the separate supports of the earlier building new supports were added, but if the foundations almost coincided they were re-used—not a very sound architectural procedure. Vitruvius says that this temple was hypaethral, but at the time he wrote it was not yet finished. Certainly a roof would have been necessary over the chryselephantine cult statue.

This third temple also seemed fated to be left incomplete. Judging by the carving of the capitals (pl. LIII, B), the eastern columns were the work of Cossutius; other capitals, not so well cut, apparently were done under Syrian kings in the time of Augustus; while still a third version of Cossutius's design resembles Hadrianic work. Sulla in 86 B.C. took some of the capitals and shafts to Rome for the Temple of Jupiter, where they had a great influence on Roman architecture.[5] It has been argued that Hadrian's capitals replaced those carried off by Sulla. At any rate, Hadrian's workmen finished the building, continuing the design of Cossutius, and it was dedicated in A.D. 131. The temple platform was walled in, an entrance gate built, and numerous statues of Hadrian dedicated by grateful cities, the most imposing being a colossus given, appropriately, by Athens.

There is no record of the destruction of the Temple of Zeus. Twenty-one columns were standing in 1450. About 1760 a Turkish governor used one for lime, and in 1852 a hurricane razed another. The first person to excavate or measure the temple was Penrose in 1846. He climbed up to the architrave after throwing a stone tied to a cord over it by which he pulled up a heavier cord to which was attached a rope ladder; this he fastened to the entablature. Beginning in 1886 the Greek Archaeological Society excavated there. A harmless hermit lived on top of the eastern group of columns, but he has gone long since, and now fifteen standing columns and one recumbent one are all that remain of this monumental building.

[5] Pliny *Natural History* XXXVI.5.

REFERENCES

The star * indicates the most important sources for the study of the temple

FRAZER, *Pausanias*, vol. II, pp. 178 ff.

GÜTSCHOW, M., "Untersuchungen zum korinthischen Kapitell, I," *Jahrb.*, XXXVI (1921), pp. 44 ff.

*PENROSE, F. C., *An Investigation of the Principles of Athenian Architecture*, London, 1888.

———, "Excavations in Greece, 1886–1887," *J.H.S.*, VIII (1887), pp. 272 ff.

*WELTER, G., "Das Olympieion in Athen," *Ath. Mitt.*, XLVII (1922), pp. 61 ff.; XLVIII (1923), pp. 182 ff.

KEY TO ABBREVIATIONS USED IN THE FOOTNOTES AND REFERENCES

Frazer, *Pausanias*—J. G. Frazer, *Pausanias's Description of Greece*, London, 1913.
Richter, *Sculpture*—G. M. A. Richter, *The Sculpture and Sculptors of the Greeks*, New Haven, 1930.
Shoe, *Profiles*—L. T. Shoe, *Profiles of Greek Mouldings*, Cambridge [Mass.], 1936.
Weickert, *Typen*—C. Weickert, *Typen der archaischen Architektur in Griechenland und Kleinasien*, Augsburg, 1929.

PERIODICALS

A. J. A.—*American Journal of Archaeology*.
Arch. Anz.—*Archäologischer Anzeiger, Beiblatt zum Jahrbuch des deutschen archäologischen Instituts*.
Ath. Mitt.—*Mitteilungen des deutschen archäologischen Instituts, Athenische Abteilung*.
B. S. A.—*The Annual of the British School at Athens*.
Jahrb.—*Jahrbuch des deutschen archäologischen Instituts*.
Jahresb.—*Jahresbericht über die Fortschritte des klassischen Altertumswissenschaft*.
J. H. S.—*The Journal of Hellenic Studies*.
Oest. Jahresh.—*Jahreshefte des österreichischen archäologischen Instituts*.
Röm. Mitt.—*Mitteilungen des deutschen archäologischen Instituts, Römische Abteilung*.

GLOSSARY

Abacus: The top member of a capital.

Adyton: The inner sanctuary, or holy of holies.

Aegis: A goatskin worn as armor over the arm and chest.

Akrolithic: Stone-tipped. In an akrolithic cult statue, usually the head, hands, and feet were of stone, the rest of wood.

Akroterion: An ornament surmounting the apex or lower angle of a pediment.

Amphiprostyle: Having a portico of columns in the front and rear only.

Anathyrosis: The system of dressing the surfaces of a block of stone or the top and bottom of a drum so that contact with the next member is made at a smooth margin only, the rest of the surface being rough and slightly cut away.

Annulet: A narrow molding in the form of a ring, especially one of the fillets used at the lower part of a Doric capital.

Anta: A corner post, or pilaster, of slight projection terminating the lateral wall of a cella and serving as respond to a column.

Antefix: An ornament at the eaves concealing the ends of the cover tiles or on the sima. Also used of ornaments on the crest of the ridge of a roof.

Architrave: The lowest member of an entablature, resting on and connecting the columns. Also called an epistyle.

Ashlar Masonry: Regular masonry of squared stone with horizontal courses and actually or approximately vertical joints.

Astragal: A small molding of round convex section, measuring generally one-half to three-quarters of a circle.

Atlantes: Male figures used as supports in the place of columns. Also called Telamones.

Balk: A roughly squared timber beam.

Bed Molding: A strip under any projecting member, especially that under the corona of a cornice.

Caryatids: Female figures used as supports in the place of columns.

Cavetto: A molding of concave section, measuring usually one-quarter of a circle.

Cella (or Naos): The enclosed sanctuary of a temple.

Chryselephantine: Made of gold and ivory. Applied to a statue made with a wooden core, gold drapery and ornaments, and ivory flesh parts.

Cornice: The upper member of an entablature, consisting of the bed molding, corona, and sima.

Corona: The projecting member of a cornice with a vertical face.

Dado: The lower portion of a wall when treated as a continuous wainscot.

Dentils: Rectangular blocks in the bed molding of an Ionic or Corinthian cornice, originally representing the ends of joists which carried a flat roof.

Dipteral: Surrounded by a double row of columns.

Distyle in Antis: Having two columns between antae.

Echinus: The convex member below the abacus in a Doric column and between the volutes of an Ionic column where it is carved with an egg and dart.

Empolia: The wooden blocks in the center of column drums holding wooden pins which centered and connected the drums together. (See p. xvi.)

Enneastyle: Having nine columns on the façade.

Entablature: The superstructure of a temple resting on the columns and composed of the architrave, frieze, and cornice.

GLOSSARY

ENTASIS: A slightly convex curve given to a column as it tapers upward to avoid the illusion of concavity that would be given if the line were made straight.

EPISTYLE: See ARCHITRAVE.

EUTHYNTERIA: The leveling course which connects the buried foundations with the visible superstructure of a building.

FASCIA: One of the flat bands into which the architraves of the Ionic and Corinthian orders are subdivided.

FILLET: A narrow, raised band with a flat profile.

FRIEZE: The middle member of an entablature, consisting in the Doric order of triglyphs and metopes and in the Ionic order of a flat band, often sculptured; also used for any flat horizontal band of sculptured or painted ornament.

GEISON: That part of a cornice consisting of the bed molding and corona.

GUILLOCHE: A plaited pattern formed by bands intertwined round circular centers.

GUTTAE: The pendent tapering cylinders, or drops, under the mutules and regulae of a Doric entablature.

HEXASTYLE: Having six columns on the façade.

HYPAETHRAL: Unroofed or open to the sky.

KYMATION: A wave molding of double curvature.

LEWIS: A contrivance for hoisting. (See p. xvi.)

LINTEL: A single piece of wood or stone placed over a window or door to support the weight above, or an architrave block over an intercolumniation.

MEGARON: The principal hall of a Mycenaean palace.

METOPE: A sunken panel between the triglyphs in the Doric order.

MUTULE: A projecting slab on the soffit of a Doric cornice.

NAOS: See CELLA.

NECKING: The upper part of the shaft of a column just below the capital, often with one or more grooves.

OCTOSTYLE: Having eight columns on the façade.

OPISTHODOMOS: The recessed rear porch of a temple.

ORTHOSTATES: The bottom course of the walls of a temple, usually two or three times higher than the upper courses.

PARAPET: A low wall or barrier built on the edge of a terrace or platform, or above a cornice.

PENTASTYLE: Having five columns on the façade.

PEPLOS: A garment worn by women and sometimes draped over the statues of goddesses.

PERIBOLOS: A sacred enclosure usually surrounded by a wall.

PERIPTERAL: Surrounded by columns.

PERISTASIS: All of the temple outside of the walls of the cella.

PERISTYLE: The covered colonnade surrounding a building or a courtyard.

PIER: A support, square or rectangular in section; a pillar.

PILASTER: A flat engaged pillar.

PODIUM: A low wall or continuous pedestal on which columns or entire temples are carried.

POROS: A kind of coarse limestone found in Greece and extensively used in building.

PRONAOS: The porch in front of the naos, or cella, of a temple.

PROÇYLAIA: A gate building, with more than one doorway, to a sacred enclosure.

PSEUDODIPTERAL: Dipteral, with the inner row of columns omitted.

PTEROMA: The passage between the walls of the cella and the peristyle.

PTERON: The wing, or flank colonnade, of a temple.

PURLIN: Horizontal timber parallel to the ridge beam to support rafters at a lower point in the sloping roof.

RAKING CORNICE: The part of the cornice over a pediment.

REGULA: A narrow strip under the taenia of a Doric architrave, as long as the triglyph above it and with guttae hanging from it.

REVETMENT: A decorative facing.

RINCEAU: An ornamental pattern of foliated branches in a curved design.

SCOTIA: A concave molding commonly used in the base of the Ionic order.

SIMA: The terracotta or marble gutter of a building.

SOCLE: A base or plinth forming the foundation for a wall, pier, column, or statue.

SOFFIT: The flat underface of an architectural member, e.g., of the architrave or the cornice.

STELE: An upright stone slab used for sculptured reliefs or painted decoration, or for an inscription—often a gravestone.

STEREOBATE: The substructure of a temple, including the stylobate.

STYLOBATE: The upper step of the stereobate forming a platform for the columns.

TAENIA: The projecting fillet which crowns the architrave of a Doric entablature.

TETRAGLYPH: A member of a Doric frieze separating the metopes, with four projections and three whole channels.

TETRASTYLE: Having four columns on the façade.

TORUS: A molding of convex profile, usually half round, occurring commonly as a member of the base of Ionic and Corinthian columns.

TRIGLYPH: A member of a Doric frieze separating the metopes, with three projections and two whole and two half channels.

VOLUTE: The spiral scroll of the Ionic capital.

PLATES

PLATE I

A. Terracotta Antefixes. In the National Museum, Athens

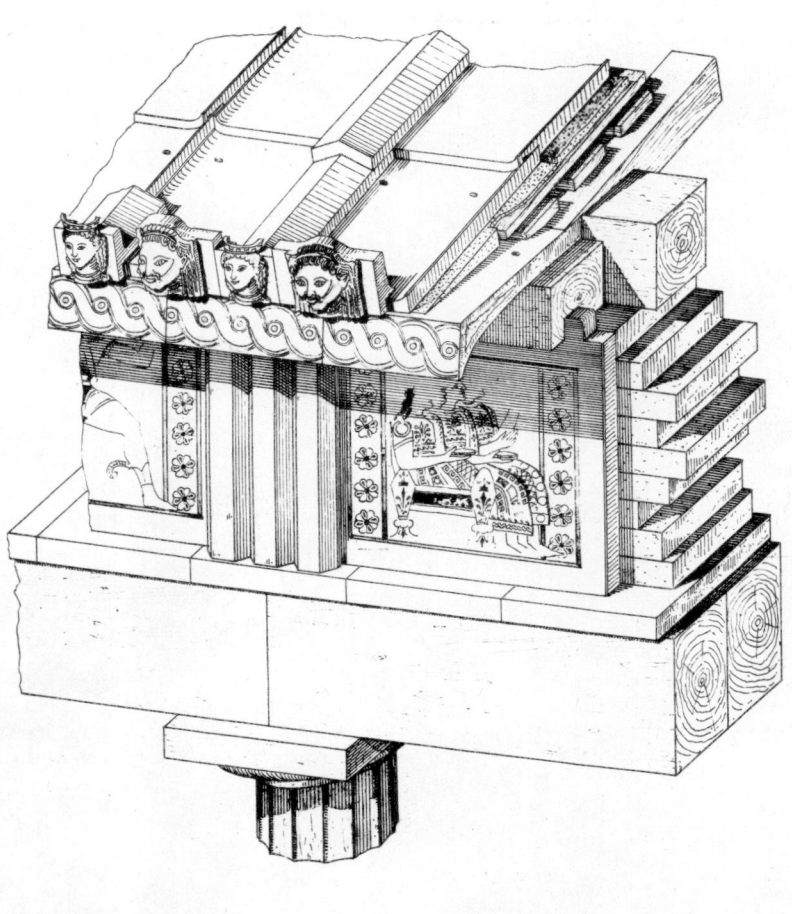

B. A Restoration of the Polychrome Entablature

C. The Present State of the Temple

THE TEMPLE OF APOLLO THERMIOS AT THERMON—DORIC

PLATE II

A. Terracotta Metope: a Hunter with Stag and Boar

B. Terracotta Metope: Perseus

C. Terracotta Metope: Seated Goddesses

D. Terracotta Metope: a Gorgon's Head

E. Terracotta Antefixes. A–E in the National Museum, Athens

THE TEMPLE OF APOLLO THERMIOS AT THERMON

PLATE III

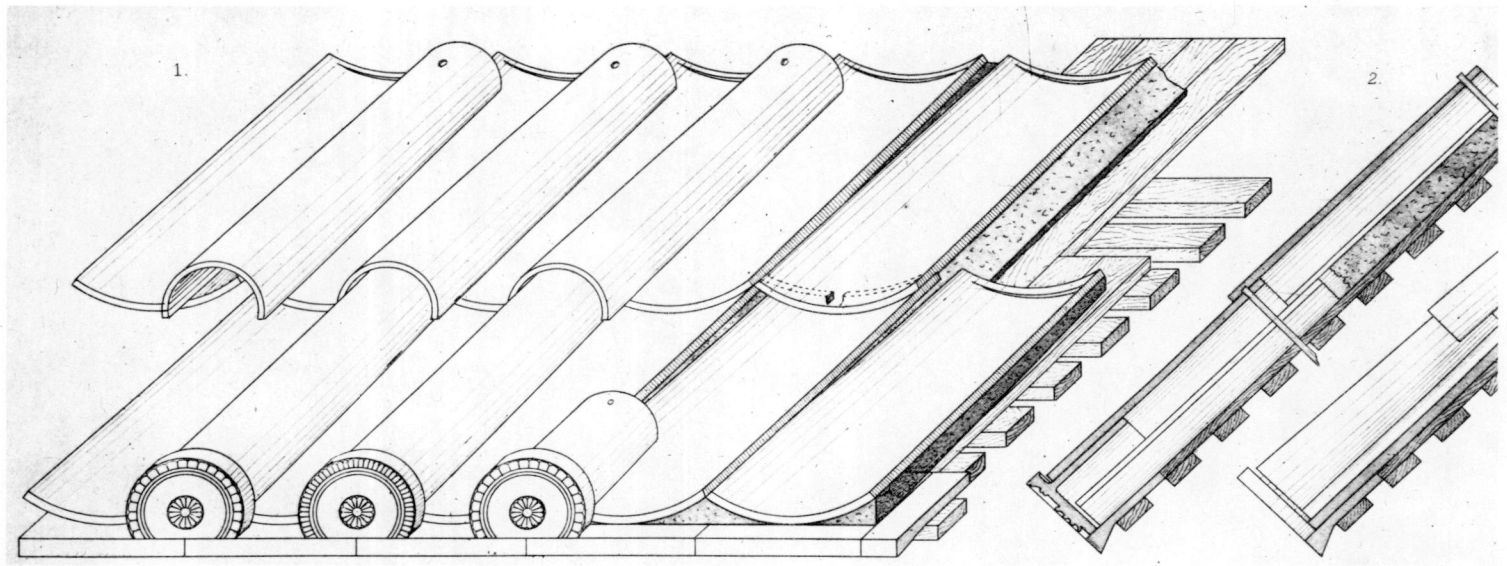

A. The Roof Construction. The Roof Was Made of Wood and Terracotta

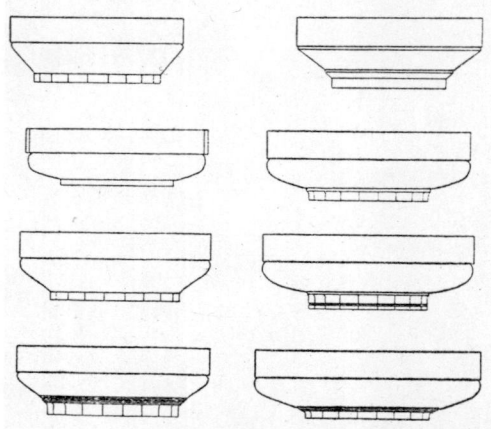

B. Types of Capitals

C. The East Façade of the Temple as Drawn by Adler

THE TEMPLE OF HERA AT OLYMPIA—DORIC

PLATE IV

A. A Restoration of a Terracotta Gable Akroterion.   B. A Head of Hera, Probably from the Cult Statue.   In the Olympia Museum

C. The Present State of the Temple

THE TEMPLE OF HERA AT OLYMPIA

PLATE V

A. A Restoration of the Western End of the Archaic Temple

B. A View of the West Portico of the Archaic Temple from the South, as Restored by F. Krischen. The Position of the Sculptured Drums Is Conjectural

THE TEMPLE OF ARTEMIS AT EPHESOS—IONIC

PLATE VI

A. Fragments of the Drums of the Archaic Temple. In the British Museum

B. A Sculptured Drum from the Later Temple. In the British Museum

C. A Restoration of the West Front of the Later Temple with the Drums Wrongly Superimposed

THE TEMPLE OF ARTEMIS AT EPHESOS

PLATE VII

A. A Restoration of the East Front. The Decoration Was Differently Arranged

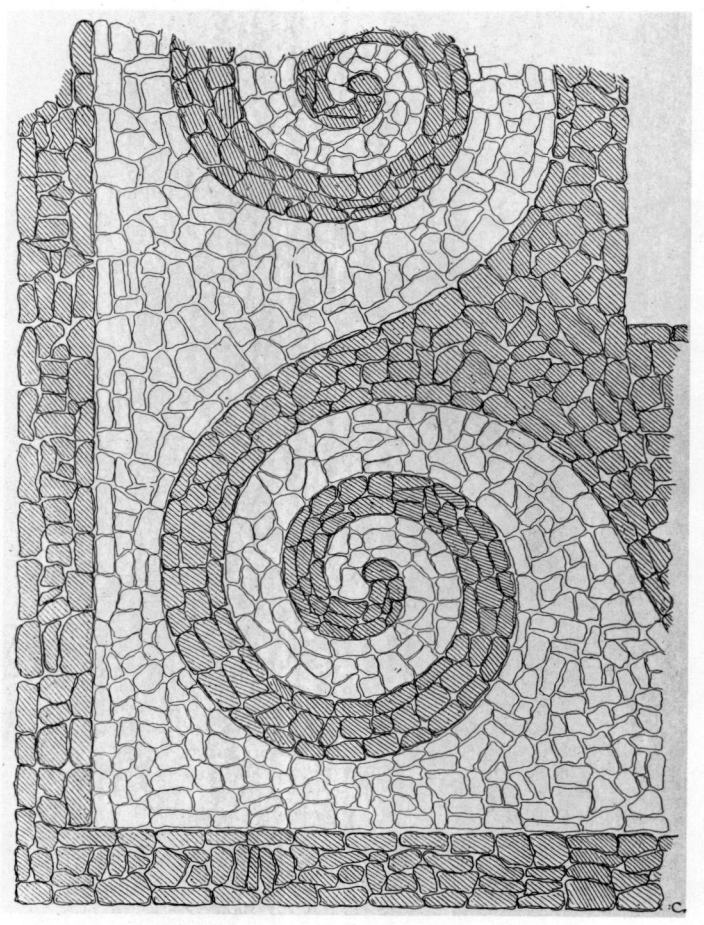

B. A Detail of the Mosaic Pavement

C. The Construction

THE TEMPLE OF ATHENA (?) AT ASSOS—DORIC

PLATE VIII

A and B. Details of the Architrave Decoration. In the Museum of Fine Arts, Boston

C. The Akropolis at Assos Seen from the Sea

THE TEMPLE OF ATHENA (?) AT ASSOS

PLATE IX

A. The Temple as Drawn by Stuart in 1751

B. The Temple as Drawn by H. W. Williams in 1818

THE TEMPLE OF APOLLO AT CORINTH—DORIC

PLATE X

A. Comparison of the Orders of the Temples of Apollo at Corinth and Delphi and the Old Temple of Athena, Athens
B. A View from the South with Restored Stereobate

C. A View from the East

THE TEMPLE OF APOLLO AT CORINTH

PLATE XI

A. A Restoration of the Early Temple in Antis, with the Outline of the Peisistratid Temple. Details of the Poros Pedimental Figures, Wrongly Placed Here, Are Shown on the Opposite Page

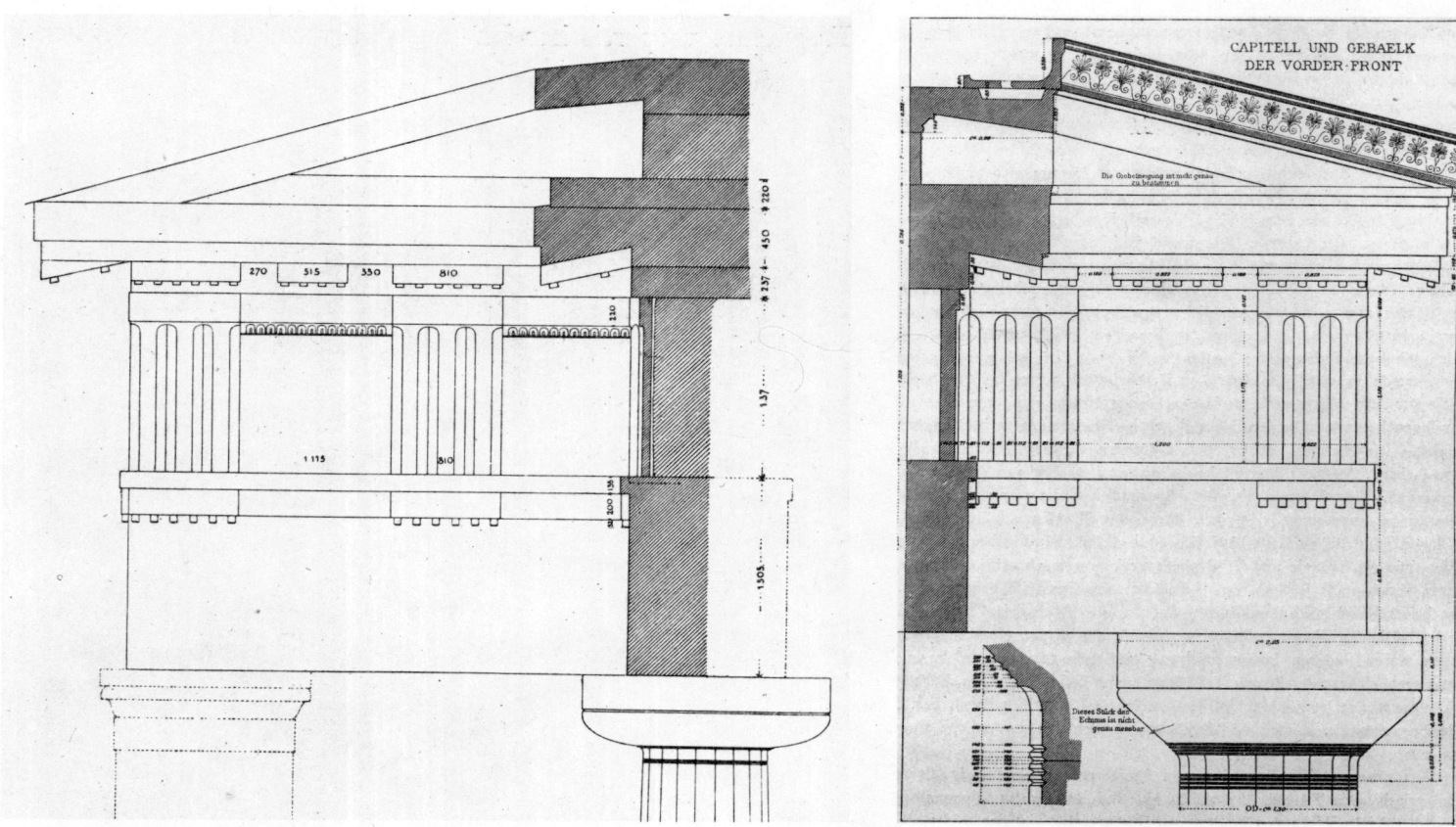

B. A Restoration of a Corner of the Small Temple in Antis.   C. A Restoration of a Corner of the Peisistratid Temple

THE OLD TEMPLE OF ATHENA ON THE AKROPOLIS AT ATHENS—DORIC

PLATE XII

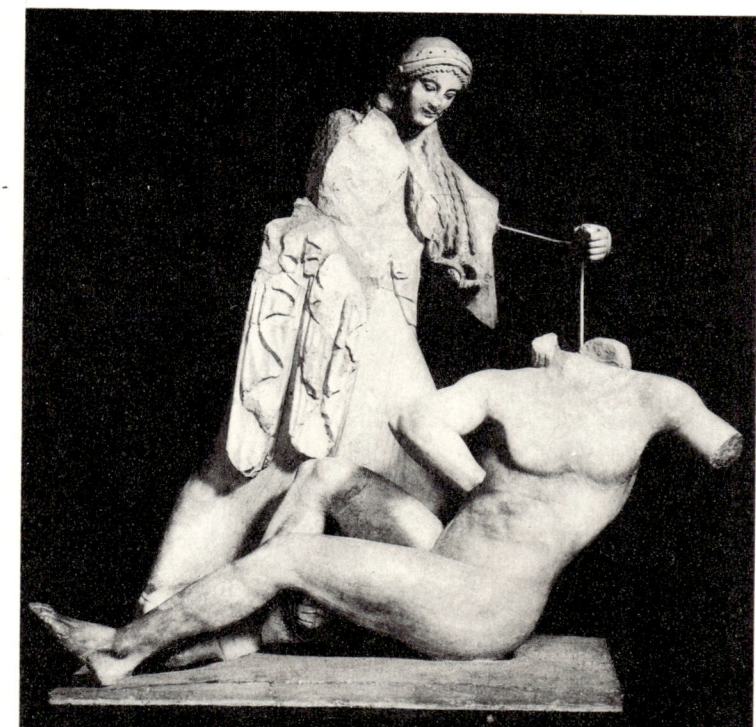

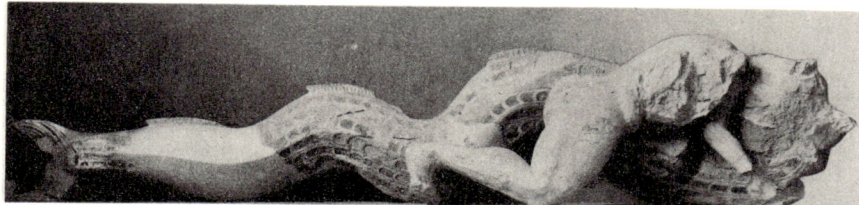

A. Athena and a Giant from the Peisistratid Temple. B. Head of a Monster. C. Herakles and the Triton. D. Head of Herakles Found in 1938. A–D in the Akropolis Museum

E. The Present State of the Temple with the Erechtheion Beyond and the City Below, Taken from the Parthenon

THE OLD TEMPLE OF ATHENA ON THE AKROPOLIS AT ATHENS

PLATE XIII

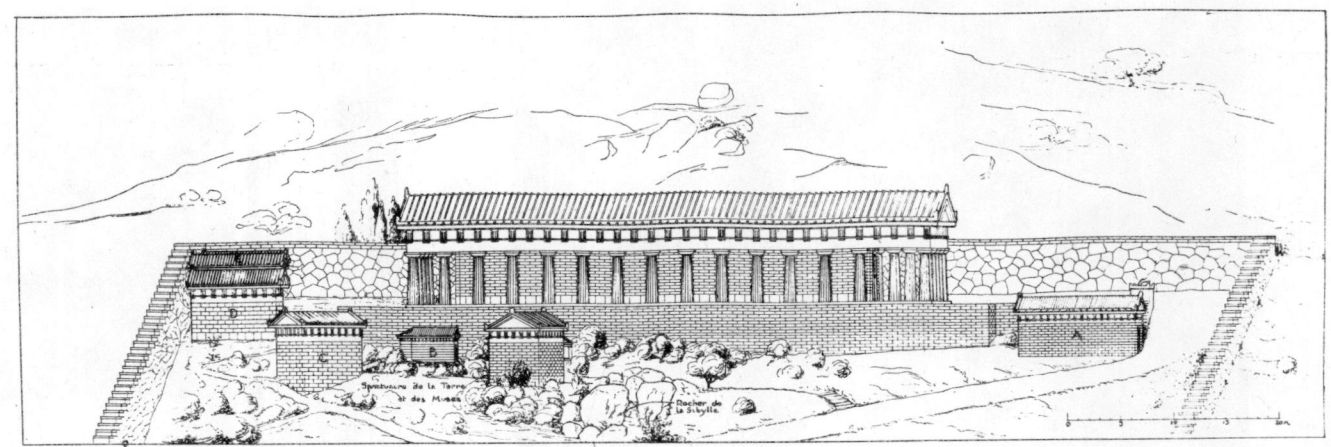
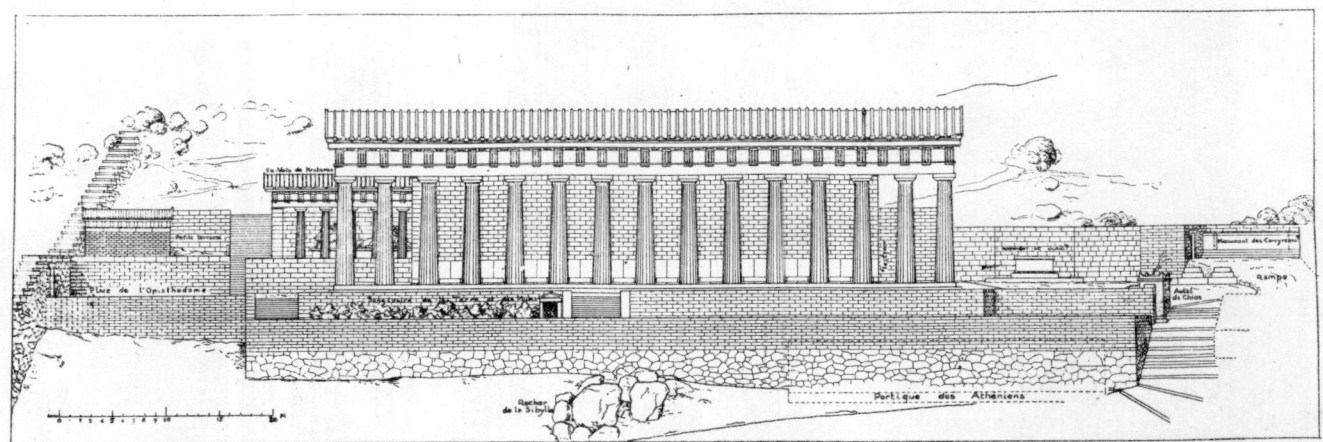

A and B. Restorations of the Temple in the Early VI Century B.C. and in the Late IV Century B.C.

C. A Model of Delphi as It Was in the II Century A.D. In the Metropolitan Museum

THE TEMPLE OF APOLLO AT DELPHI—DORIC

PLATE XIV

A. A Lion Devouring a Hind, from the East Pediment of the Alkmeonid Temple. In the Delphi Museum. B. Akroterion (center) and Figures from the East Pediment of the Alkmeonid Temple. In the Delphi Museum

C. A View of the Remains of the Temple from Mount Parnassos

THE TEMPLE OF APOLLO AT DELPHI

PLATE XV

A. A Restoration of the East Front and a Section through the Pediment.   B. The Construction

THE TEMPLE OF APHAIA AT AIGINA—DORIC

PLATE XVI

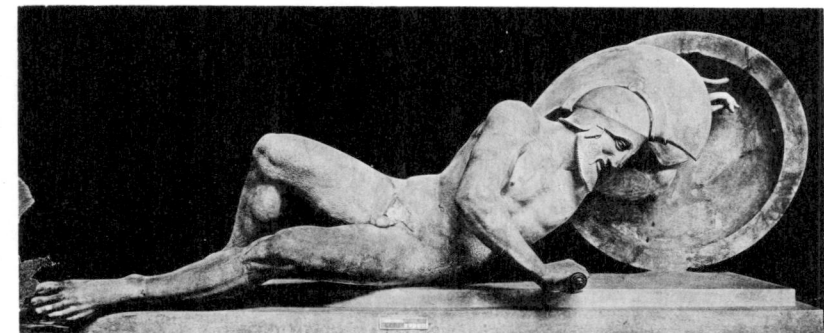

A. Athena, from the West Pediment.   B. Herakles, from the East Pediment.   C. A Fallen Warrior, from the East Pediment
A–C in the Glyptothek, Munich

D. The Interior of the Temple

THE TEMPLE OF APHAIA AT AIGINA

PLATE XVII

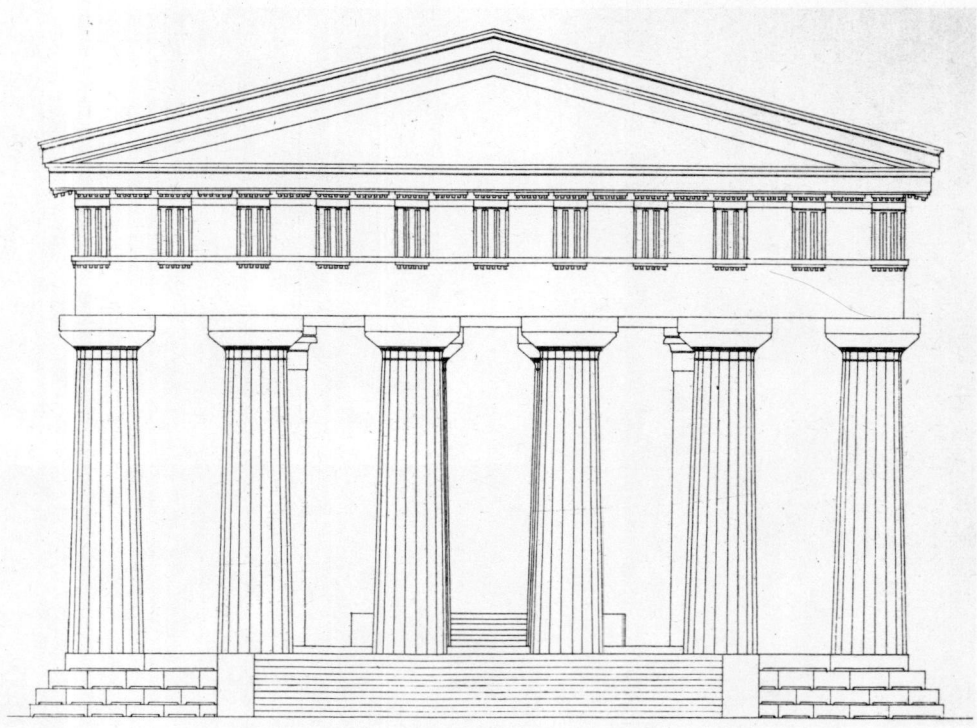

A. A Restoration of the East Front

B. A Metope: the Marriage of Zeus and Hera. In the Museo Nazionale, Palermo

THE TEMPLE OF HERA, OR THE TEMPLE E-R, AT SELINUS—DORIC

PLATE XVIII

A. A Metope: Herakles Fighting an Amazon. In the Museo Nazionale, Palermo

B. The Present State of the Temple

THE TEMPLE OF HERA, OR THE TEMPLE E-R, AT SELINUS

PLATE XIX

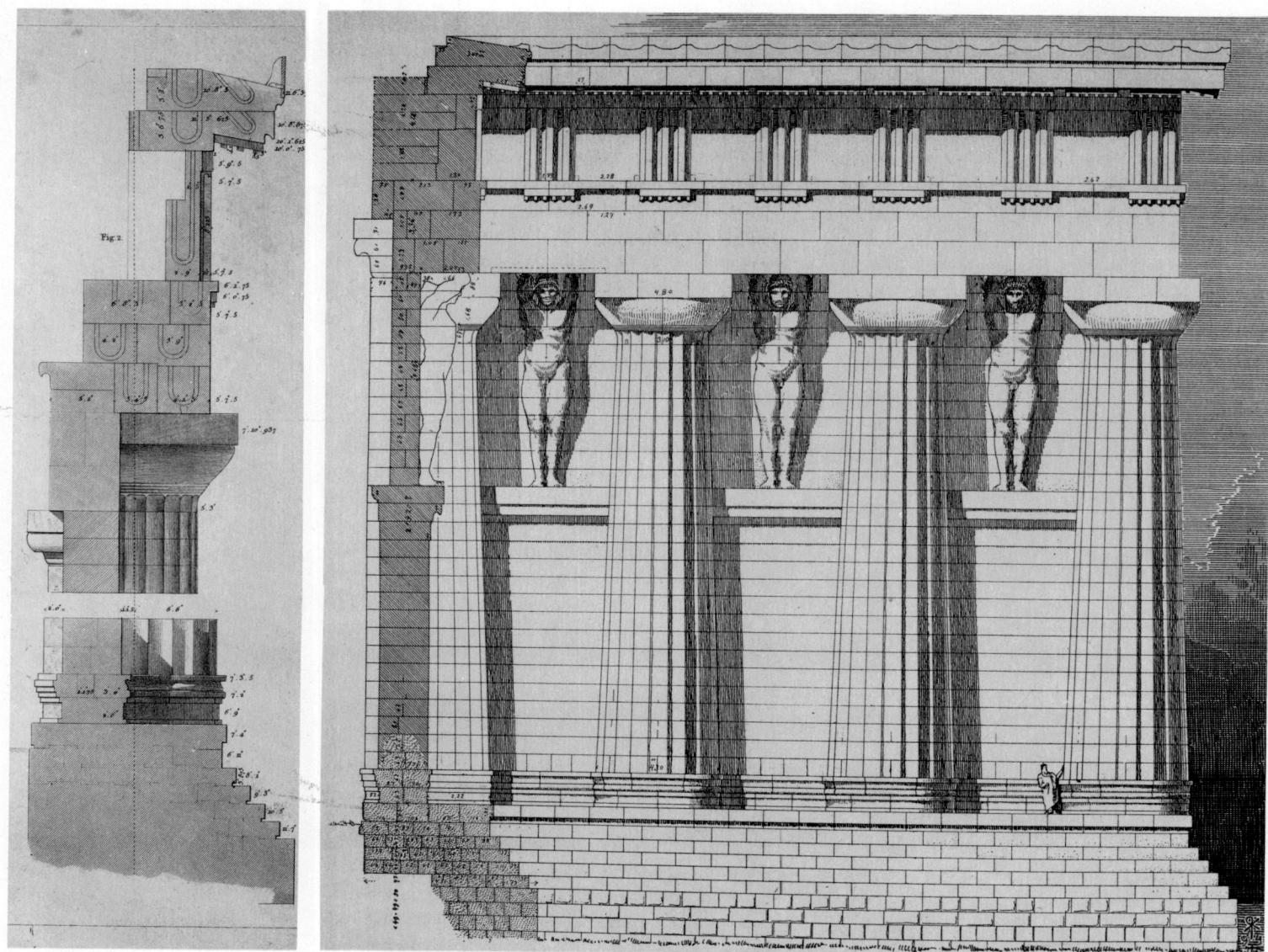

A. A Section Showing the Inner Pilasters and the Means of Hoisting Blocks. B. A Restoration of a Corner of the Temple Showing the Position of the Colossal Figures

C. A Restoration of the Façade by Cockerell Showing the Comparative Sizes of this Temple and the Parthenon. The Exact Height Is Conjectural

THE TEMPLE OF ZEUS OLYMPIOS AT AKRAGAS (AGRIGENTUM)—DORIC

PLATE XX

A. Part of the North Side of the Temple at the End of the XIX Century.   B. The Head of One of the Colossal Figures

C. An Atlante and Corner of the North Wall of the Temple

THE TEMPLE OF ZEUS OLYMPIOS AT AKRAGAS

A. The East Pediment as Restored by Studniczka. The Sculptures Are in the Olympia Museum

B. The West Pediment as Restored by Treu. The Sculptures Are in the Olympia Museum

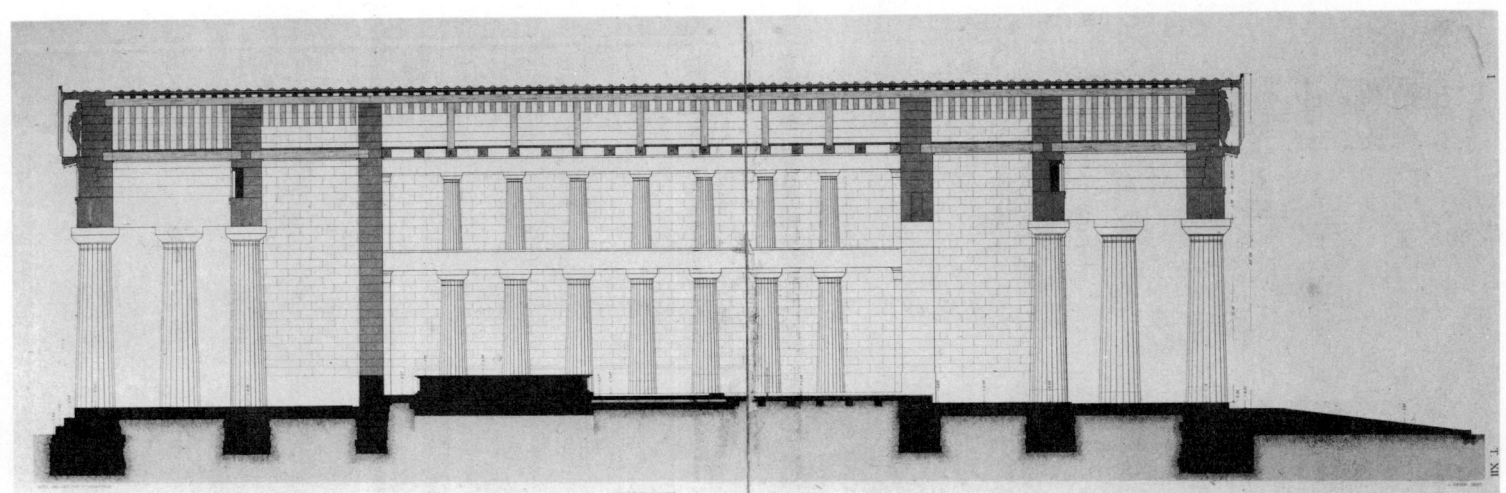

C. Longitudinal Section

D. A Model of Olympia as It Appeared in the II Century A.D. In the Metropolitan Museum

THE TEMPLE OF ZEUS AT OLYMPIA—DORIC

PLATE XXII

A. A Corner of the Entablature Showing the Roof Construction. B. Restorations of the East Front and of the Interior Showing the Conjectural Appearance of the Cult Statue

C. The Present State of the Temple

THE TEMPLE OF ZEUS AT OLYMPIA

PLATE XXIII

A. The Central Group from the West Pediment: Theseus and a Centaur, Apollo, Deidameia and Eurytion. In the Olympia Museum

B–E. Figures from the East Pediment: "Handmaiden," "Seer," "Alpheios," "Kladeos." In the Olympia Museum

THE TEMPLE OF ZEUS AT OLYMPIA

PLATE XXIV

A–D. Metopes: Herakles and Atlas, the Augean Stable, Herakles and Kerberos, the Stymphalian Birds. In the Olympia Museum

E. Lion-head Waterspouts. In the Olympia Museum

THE TEMPLE OF ZEUS AT OLYMPIA

PLATE XXV

A. The Interior, Showing the Second Range of Columns

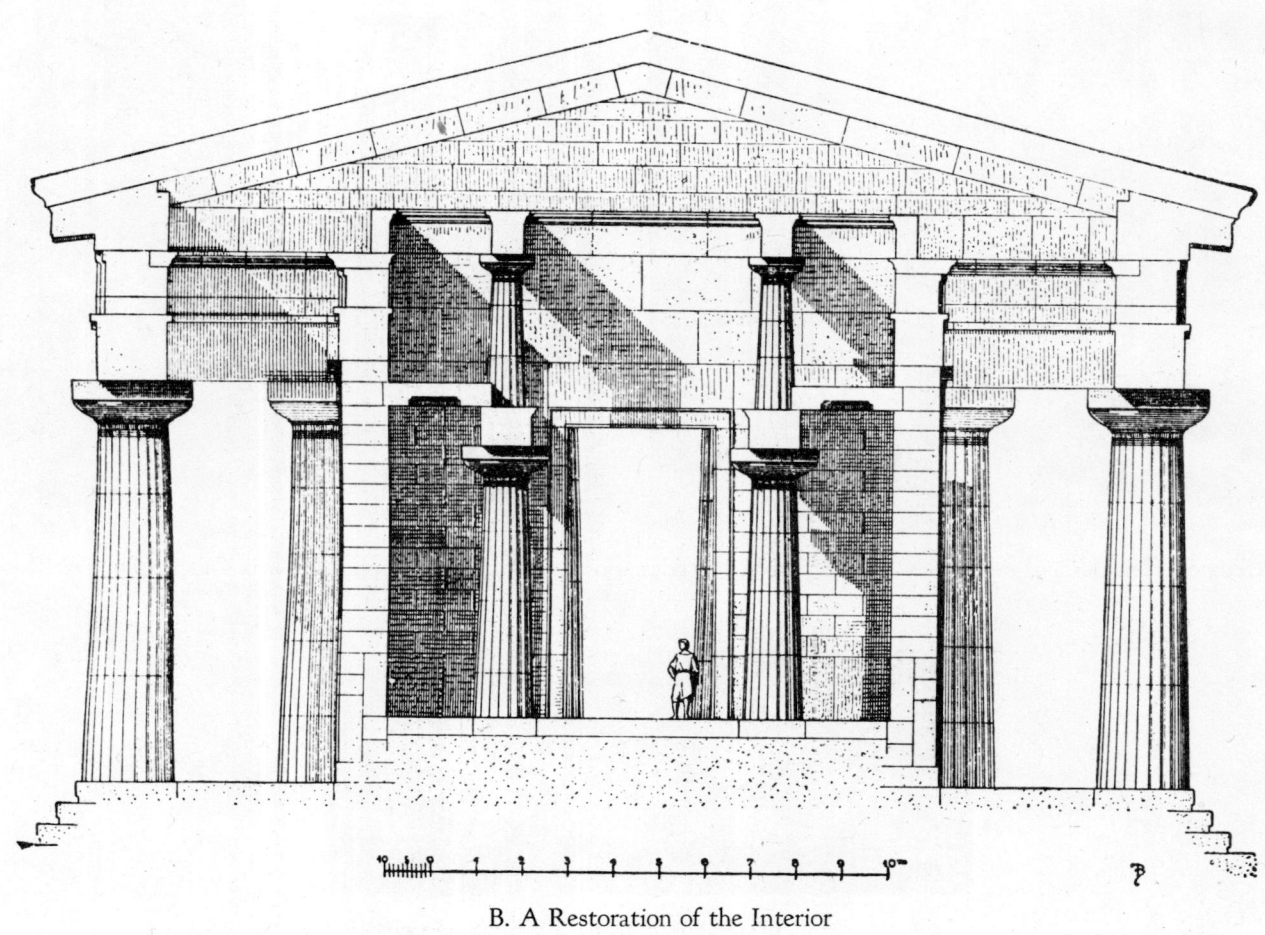

B. A Restoration of the Interior

THE "TEMPLE OF POSEIDON" AT POSEIDONIA (PAESTUM)—DORIC

PLATE XXVI

A. A View of a Corner of the "Basilica" and the Temple

B. The Present State of the Temple

THE "TEMPLE OF POSEIDON" AT POSEIDONIA

PLATE XXVII

A. A Restoration of the Interior by Dinsmoor

B. The Raking Sima. C. A Detail of the Centaur Frieze. D. Herakles, a Detail of the Amazon Frieze. B–D in the British Museum

THE TEMPLE OF APOLLO EPIKOURIOS AT BASSAI (NEAR PHIGALEIA)—DORIC

PLATE XXVIII

A. The Present State of the Interior

B. A Restoration of the Interior by Cockerell

C. The Present State of the Temple

THE TEMPLE OF APOLLO EPIKOURIOS AT BASSAI

PLATE XXIX

A. A Restored Perspective of the Portico Interior Showing the Frieze

B and C. Metopes: Herakles and the Cretan Bull, in situ; Theseus and Kerkyon, from a Cast

D. A Detail of the Frieze.   From a Cast

THE TEMPLE OF HEPHAISTOS AT ATHENS (THE THESEION)—DORIC

PLATE XXX

A. The East Front

B. The Temple from the Northwest

THE TEMPLE OF HEPHAISTOS AT ATHENS

PLATE XXXI

A. The East Pediment, the Birth of Athena (above), and the West Pediment, the Contest of Athena and Poseidon, as Drawn in 1674.

B. A Corner Showing a Metope and an Antefix in Place.   C. An Athenian Coin of about 200 B.C. with the Head of Athena Parthenos
D. The Varvakeion Statuette, a Copy of the Athena Parthenos in the National Museum, Athens

THE PARTHENON AT ATHENS—DORIC

PLATE XXXII

A. A View from the Southeast

B. A Detail of the Temple Showing the Position of the Frieze

THE PARTHENON AT ATHENS

PLATE XXXIII

A and B. Figures from the East Pediment. Right, the "Fates"

C. "Theseus," from the East Pediment   D. A Group from the West Pediment. In situ

E and F. Metopes: Scenes from the Battle of the Lapiths and Centaurs. A–C, E, F Are in the British Museum

THE PARTHENON AT ATHENS

PLATE XXXIV

A. Seated Gods from the East Frieze

B. Marshal and Maidens from the East Frieze

C. Elders from the North Frieze

D. Offering Bearers from the North Frieze

E. Young Horsemen from the North Frieze

F. Riders from the West Frieze. In situ

A, C, and D in the Akropolis Museum, B in the Louvre, E in the British Museum

THE PARTHENON AT ATHENS

PLATE XXXV

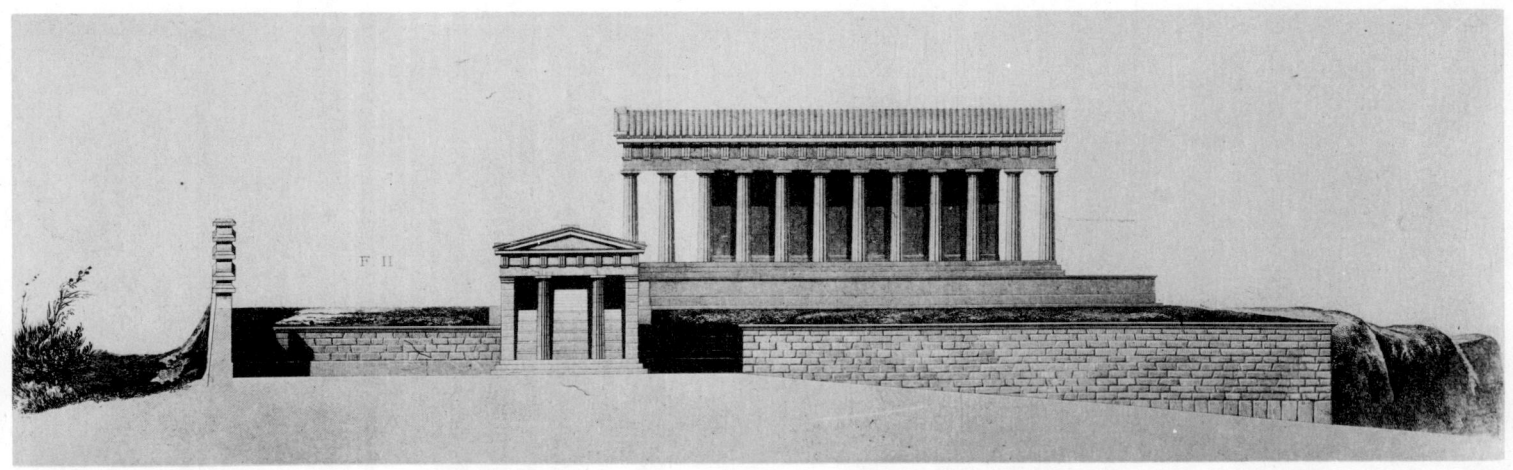

A and B. The Side and Front Elevations Restored

C. The Frieze and Architrave over an Anta Capital and the Exterior Entablature and Capital

THE TEMPLE OF POSEIDON AT SOUNION—DORIC

PLATE XXXVI

A. A View of the Temple from the Northwest.

B. A Seated Figure, Probably from a Pediment

C. Looking toward the Sea from the Interior

THE TEMPLE OF POSEIDON AT SOUNION

PLATE XXXVII

A. The Southeast Corner of the Temple

B. The Interior, Looking West

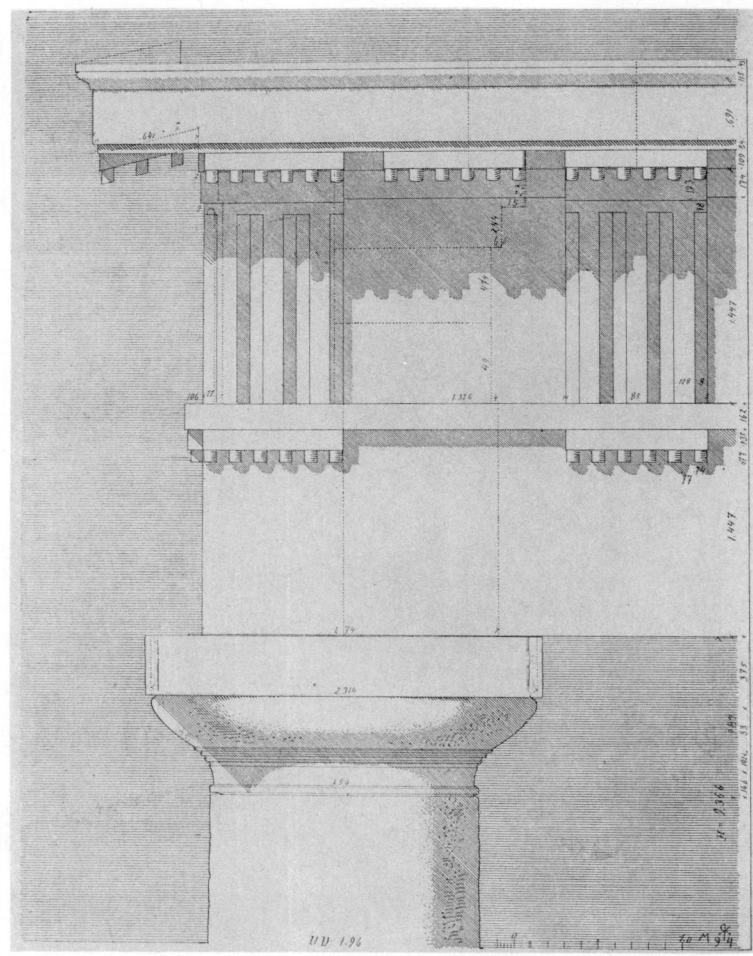

C. A Corner of the Temple as Drawn by Hittorff

THE TEMPLE AT EGESTA (SEGESTA)—DORIC

PLATE XXXVIII

A. A View into the Interior from the Southwest Corner

B. A Detail Showing the Bosses and the Curvature of the Stylobate on the South Side

C. The West Front of the Temple

THE TEMPLE AT EGESTA

PLATE XXXIX

A. The Assembly of Deities, Part of the Frieze. In situ

B and C. Two Nikes from the Parapet Built around the Temple. In the Akropolis Museum

THE TEMPLE OF ATHENA NIKE AT ATHENS—IONIC

PLATE XL

A. A Restoration of the Akropolis Showing the Position of the Temple

B. The Temple as It Appeared in 1940

THE TEMPLE OF ATHENA NIKE AT ATHENS

PLATE XLI

A. A Restoration of the East Front

B. A Restored Cross Section Showing the Statue of Hera

THE ARGIVE HERAION—DORIC

PLATE XLII

A. A Restoration of the Sima

 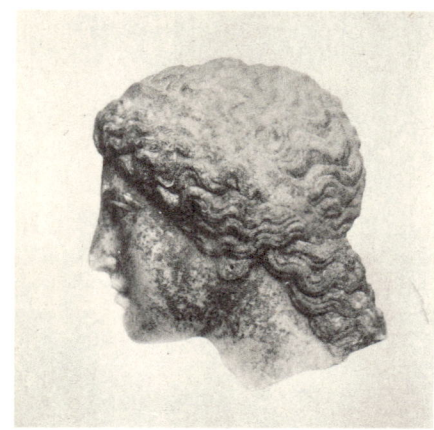

B. An Argive Coin with the Head of Hera. C. A Head of Hera, Probably from the West Pediment. In the National Museum, Athens

D. The Present State of the Temple

THE ARGIVE HERAION

PLATE XLIII

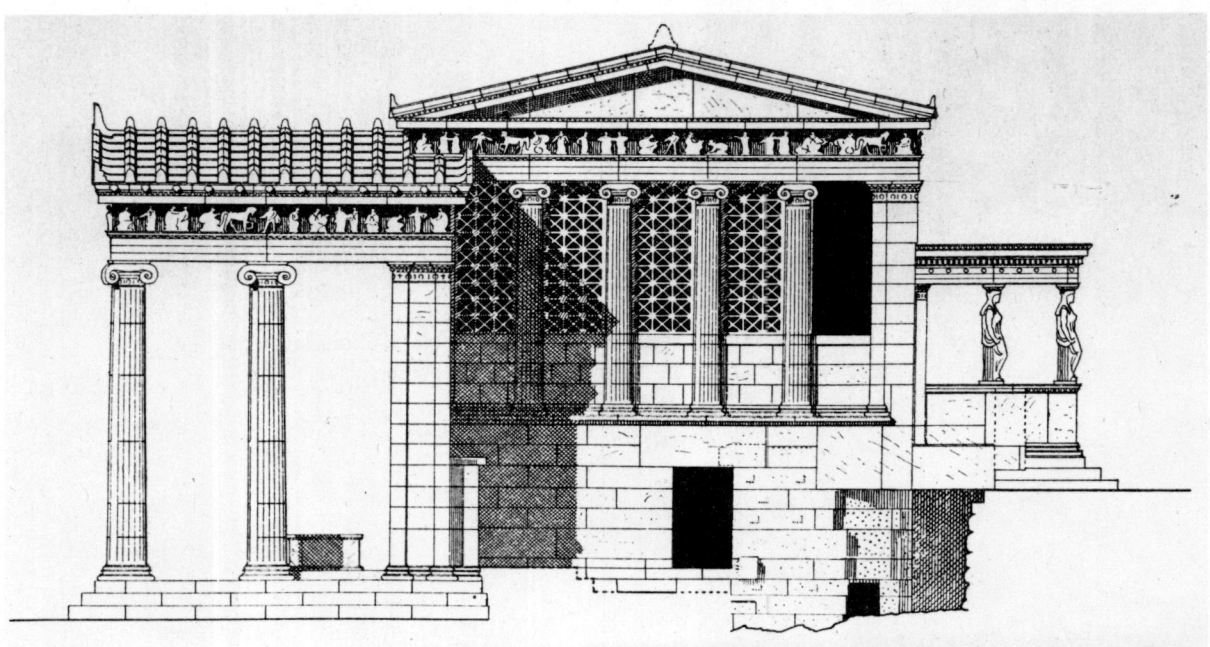

A–C. Restorations of the Temple: East Façade, West Façade, North Façade

THE ERECHTHEION AT ATHENS—IONIC

PLATE XLIV

A. A Group from the Frieze. In the Akropolis Museum, Athens.   B. The Caryatid Porch

C. The Present State of the Temple Seen from the West

THE ERECHTHEION AT ATHENS

PLATE XLV

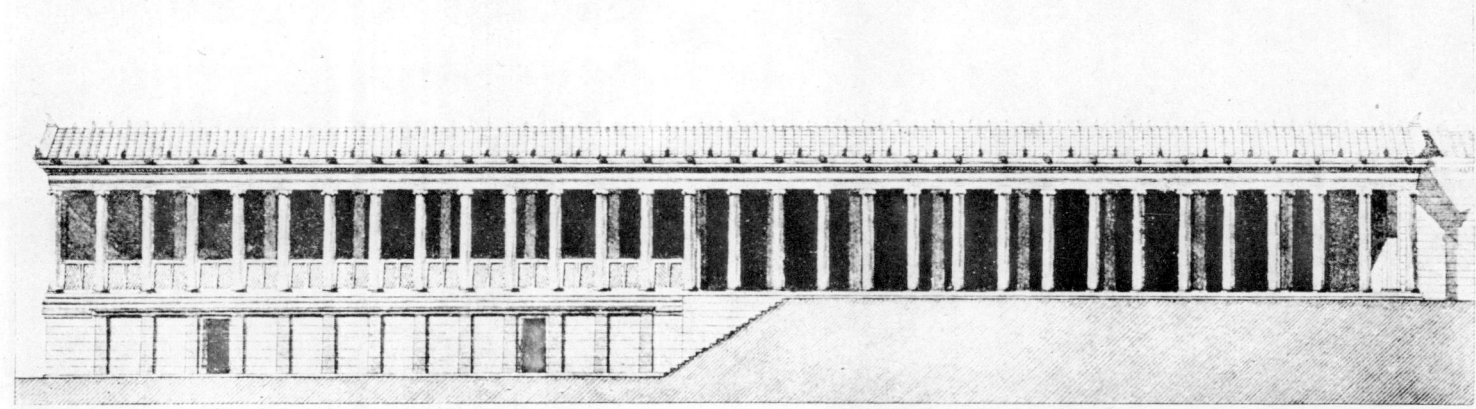

A. The Abaton, or Dormitory for Pilgrims

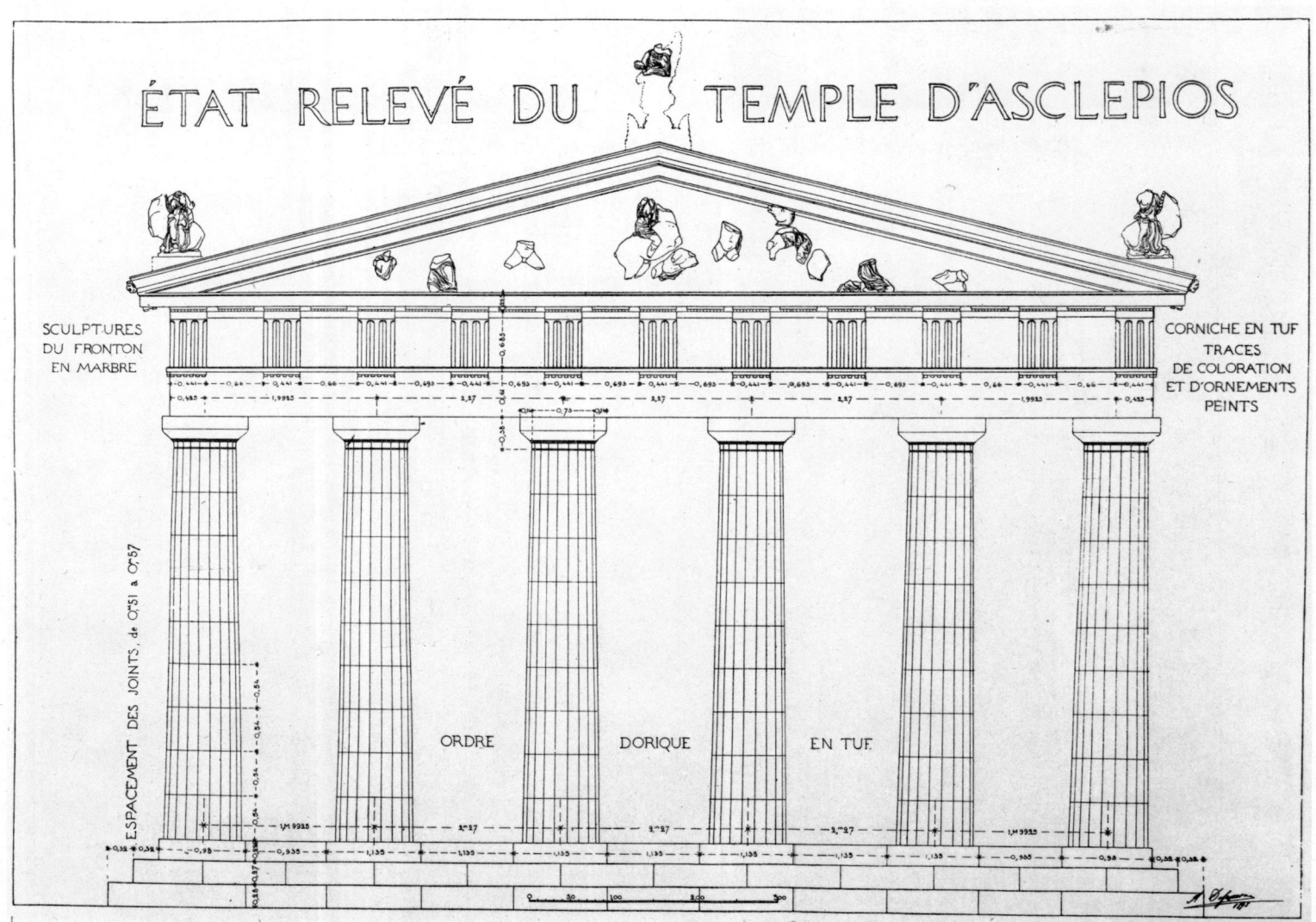

B. A Restoration of the East Front

THE TEMPLE OF ASKLEPIOS AT EPIDAUROS—DORIC

PLATE XLVI

A. A Relief of Asklepios. In the National Museum, Athens.   B. A Nike: An Akroterion. In the National Museum, Athens

C. The Theater at Epidauros with the Ruins of the Sanctuary in the Distance at the Left

THE TEMPLE OF ASKLEPIOS AT EPIDAUROS

PLATE XLVII

A. A Drawing of the East Façade

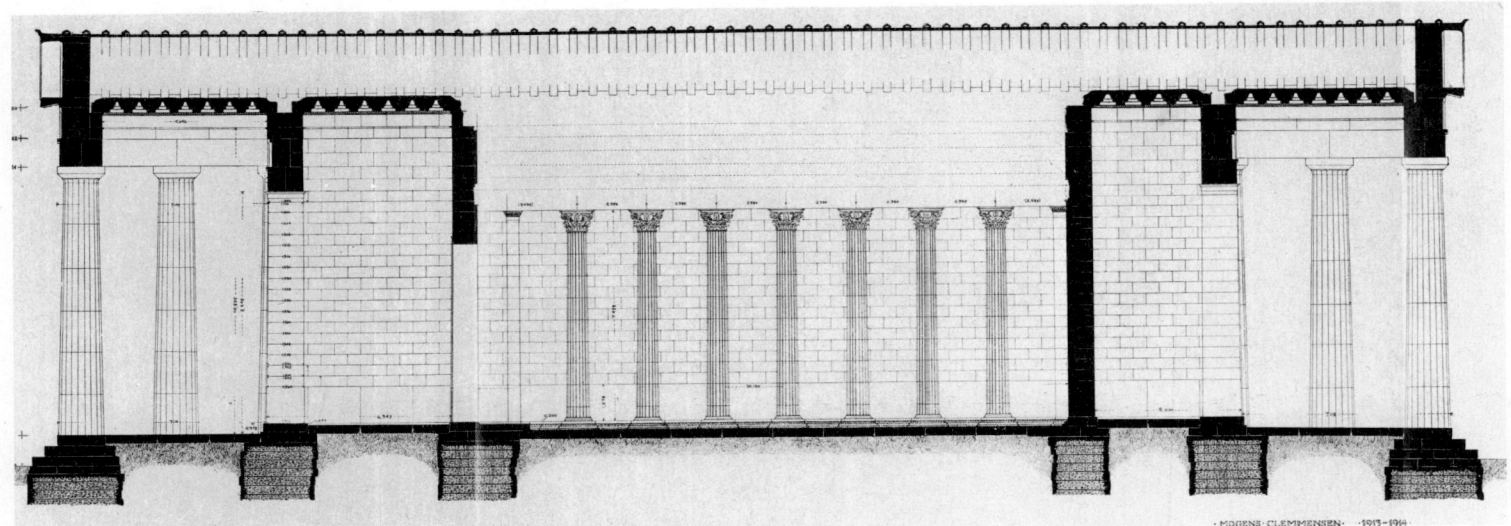

B. Longitudinal Section

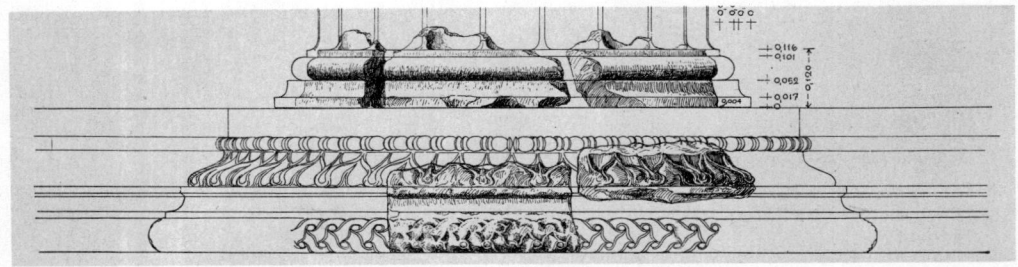

C. A Restoration of a Column Base and Base Molding in the Interior

THE TEMPLE AT ATHENA ALEA AT TEGEA—DORIC

PLATE XLVIII

A. The Head of Herakles from the West Pediment. From a Cast.   B. A Capital from the Interior, Restored

C and D. The Crowning Molding inside the Cella and the Sima.   A–D. Originals in the Museum of Tegea

E. A View of the Temple from the East

THE TEMPLE OF ATHENA ALEA AT TEGEA

PLATE XLIX

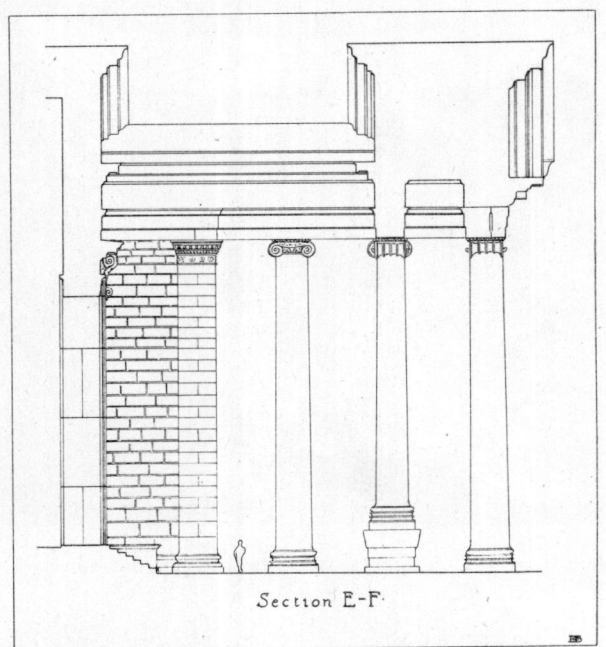
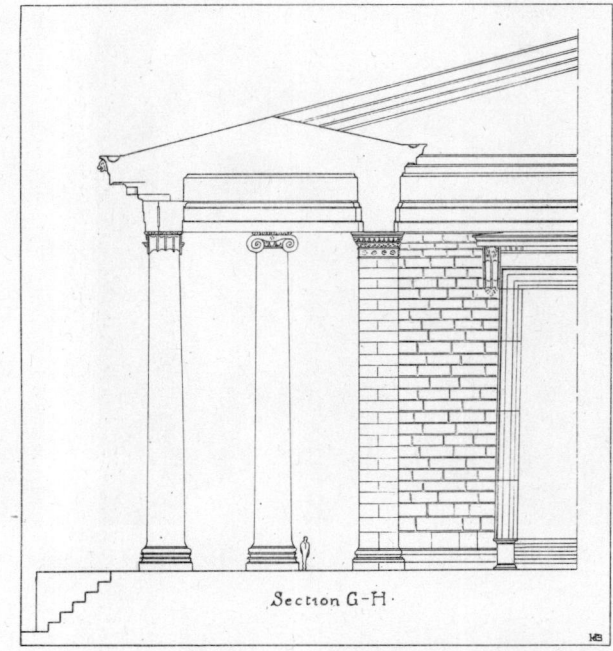

A and B. A Restoration of the East End: Longitudinal Section and Transverse Section

C. A Suggested Restoration of the West Steps

D. A Restoration of the Doorway.   E. A Detail of One of the Columns

THE TEMPLE OF ARTEMIS AT SARDIS—IONIC

PLATE L

A. A View of the East Porch from the North

B. A View of the East Porch from the Northeast

C. The Southeast Anta and the East Wall of the Cella

D. Fragments of the Anta Capital

E. A View of Sardis while the Temple Was Being Excavated

THE TEMPLE OF ARTEMIS AT SARDIS

PLATE LI

A. A Restoration Showing the Separate Shrine within the Temple Walls. B. Restored Capital and Entablature

C–E. Sculptured Column Bases from the Main Façade. C and E. In Situ, D in the Louvre

F. The Temple as It Appeared after the French Excavations in 1896

THE TEMPLE OF APOLLO AT DIDYMA—IONIC

PLATE LII

A. The Entrance to the Antechamber from the Cella

B. The Cella

THE TEMPLE OF APOLLO AT DIDYMA

PLATE LIII

A. A Restoration of a Corner. The Cornice Is Conjectural

B. Details of a Column

C. A View of the Temple after Stuart and Revett. About 1753

THE TEMPLE OF ZEUS OLYMPIOS AT ATHENS—CORINTHIAN

PLATE LIV

A. A View from the Southeast

B. A View from the Southwest

THE TEMPLE OF ZEUS OLYMPIOS AT ATHENS

1,000 COPIES OF THIS BOOK WERE PRINTED IN
AUGUST, 1943 BY THE PLANTIN PRESS, NEW YORK.
THE COLLOTYPE PLATES BY THE ULLMAN COMPANY,
BROOKLYN, N. Y.